Soft Skills for Kids

Soft Skills for Kids

In Schools, at Home, and Online

2nd Edition

Nancy Armstrong Melser

ROWMAN & LITTLEFIELD
Lanham • Boulder • New York • London

Published by Rowman & Littlefield
An imprint of The Rowman & Littlefield Publishing Group, Inc.
4501 Forbes Boulevard, Suite 200, Lanham, Maryland 20706
www.rowman.com

86-90 Paul Street, London EC2A 4NE, United Kingdom

British Library Cataloguing in Publication Information Available

Library of Congress Cataloging-in-Publication Data

Names: Melser, Nancy Armstrong, author.
Title: Soft skills for kids : in schools, at home, and online / Nancy Armstrong Melser.
Other titles: Soft skills for children
Description: Second edition. | Lanham : Rowman & Littlefield, [2022] | Includes
    bibliographical references. | Summary: "Soft skills help prepare kids for school and
    the workplace. They are a series of strategies that help children learn competencies
    such as manners, respect, and organization. This book focuses on fourteen soft skills
    that all kids need, as well as how teachers and parents can work together to help
    children both at home and in educational settings"—Provided by publisher.
Identifiers: LCCN 2021055960 (print) | LCCN 2021055961 (ebook) | ISBN
    9781475864885 (cloth) | ISBN 9781475864892 (paperback) | ISBN
    9781475864908 (epub)
Subjects: LCSH: Social learning. | Soft skills—Study and teaching. | Life skills—Study
    and teaching. | Education—Parent participation.
Classification: LCC LC192.4 .M45 2022 (print) | LCC LC192.4 (ebook) | DDC
    303.3/2—dc23/eng/20220218
LC record available at https://lccn.loc.gov/2021055960
LC ebook record available at https://lccn.loc.gov/2021055961

Contents

Preface

Soft skills is a catch phrase in the world of business. Numerous websites and books exist on the topic of soft skills as they apply to career searches and job preparedness. Employers are looking for well-rounded applicants who know the *hard skills* or background information and technical skills that are necessary for jobs. However, they are also looking for employees who have *soft skills* as well.

According to Dictionary.com, soft skills are defined as "personal attributes that enable someone to interact effectively and harmoniously with other people." As a teacher educator for almost thirty years, I noticed that while the majority of my pre-service teachers were wonderful and well prepared, there were always a handful of students who were missing soft skills in the field of teaching. These future teachers were sometimes lacking in confidence, professionalism, and a good work ethic.

After working with future teachers who were deficient in professional and people skills, I decided to give a survey to school superintendents and administrators about what was lacking in today's pre-service teachers. One respondent simply stated, "Soft Skills." Curious about this answer I began researching soft skills as they applied to teachers. I completed presentations and wrote my first book titled *Teaching Soft Skills in a Hard World: Skills for Beginning Teachers.*

A week after submitting my book for publication, I received an email from a state legislator announcing a new requirement for K-12 students for employment and future job skills. In this email, the term *soft skills* was mentioned once again, but this time, they applied to children. As a teacher and parent, I was immediately interested in this idea as it applies to school-age students and wanted to embark on another book that applied to this demographic group.

I once again studied the term *soft skills* and found that it applied mostly to the business world, and not to children. After much research and exploration of the idea of soft skills with children, I wrote a second book titled *Soft Skills for Children: A Guide for Parents and Teachers*. This book was published in January of 2019, and covered many of the soft skills that are important to teach children, both at home and at school.

However, just a few months later, the COVID-19 pandemic hit our world and impacted children in a variety of ways. They were suddenly sent home from schools, forced to learn in an online environment, and parents suddenly became teachers as well. The pandemic of 2020 created a whole new use for soft skills in children as both teachers and parents were now working together to instruct students in online and hybrid environments. Families were suddenly setting up home classrooms, parents were learning how to log students into online formats, and teachers were scrambling to create lessons that would cover the required curriculum and also help children with their anxiety and loss of classroom instruction.

This book was revised to assist teachers and parents in applying the soft skills from the first book into an online setting as well. As more and more families are learning from home, whether through a hybrid model of in-class instruction and online learning sponsored by school systems, or through homeschooling where parents intentionally plan and teach curriculum to their students, the soft skills presented here will play an even bigger role than they did just two years ago. As Loveless (2021) stated:

> When sudden change occurs, or unanticipated problems arise, it can leave some students unable to effectively respond. As students learn to be more adaptable, they become better situated to respond to a wide range of problems. A student who learns how to adapt quickly to changing school conditions is better suited to responding in the workplace when new problems arise.

Kids have been through a lot! They have survived the physical threat of a pandemic and looming illness in their family and friends. Some have been out of school for months without seeing classmates and teachers, and are experiencing anxiety about returning to schools, continuing online education, and possibly being behind academically due to the interruptions in learning. They need to have teachers and parents who will work together to help them learn to the best of their abilities for the hard skills such as math and reading, but will also need to see teachers and parents who practice respect and composure through these changes as well.

As a teacher, I know that soft skills are used in the classroom, whether in person or online. When teachers model respectful behaviors, show students how to respond appropriately, and use strategies that incorporate the skills needed for tomorrow's careers, they are teaching soft skills that children will use for their future. The sections I included in this book for educators outline ways to incorporate soft skills into classrooms.

As a parent, I also know that soft skills are important at home. When my son and his friends shared concerns with me, told me about what kids were dealing with, and how their parents helped them through situations, I knew that soft skills were important for parents to teach as well. Also, when the pandemic occurred and many parents suddenly had to help with schooling at home, I realized that the integration of online learning would be a valuable tool as well.

I would like to offer two side notes about the information presented in this book. First, while I address *parents* in each chapter, I realize that this goes beyond just birth parents, and includes family members, step-parents, grand-parents, and honestly, anyone who is an adult figure in the lives of children. It is my belief that anyone who is willing to help a child become a more competent, well-rounded individual is welcomed to participate!

I also use the terms *kids and children* throughout the book. In my house, anyone that is living under my roof is considered a child, from preschool until they obtain jobs and are not living in my basement! *Children* is simply a word that is understood by readers that both parents and teachers can identify with.

By working in collaboration, both parents and teachers can concentrate their efforts on the soft skills that are needed in tomorrow's jobs. Using soft skills will educate children about the ways to get along with others, have attributes that will help them be successful in life, and learn strategies for successful careers in the future. By learning soft skills as children, they will be able to make the world a better place—one skill at a time.

Acknowledgments

First, I would like to acknowledge all of the children, teachers, and parents who learned and taught online during the COVID-19 pandemic. It is because of the resilience and perseverance of all of you that I wrote a second edition of the book to cover soft skills in an online environment. A special shout out to my younger friends, Nick, Elaina, and Liesl, who allowed me to use their stories in this edition.

I would also like to thank my friends Charlotte, Julie, Jeanni, and Nancy, for inspiring me to write books and follow my dreams. The Girls of the Crazy Eights also provided much support and encouragement for me during the pandemic and my own online teaching.

To my family— my son, Tyler, my mother, Joan, and my cousin Sue— thank you for your love and support each time I enter a new adventure.

Finally, to my brother, Bruce, who is fighting a battle with cancer. This is dedicated to you for being a model of resiliency and a positive attitude, even in tough times.

Introduction

Kids today are growing up in a world of uncertainty. The ever-changing political climate, fear of mass shootings in their own schools, and issues such as cyberbullying and civil unrest are taking over their once *safe havens.* In addition, the COVID-19 pandemic of 2020 brought with it challenges for children, teachers, and parents as they suddenly went into quarantine, watched their schools shut down, and instruction become virtual through online lessons and instruction. Kids quickly went to learning from home, having parents as co-teachers, and not being able to see their friends and grandparents for several months. They went through periods of anxiety and loneliness and missed major school experiences such as proms, graduations, and sporting events.

In a recent report by the National Association of School Psychologists about helping children cope with the changes due to COVID-19, they state:

> It is very important to remember that children look to adults for guidance on how to react to stressful events. Acknowledging some level of concern, without panicking, is appropriate and can result in taking the necessary actions that reduce the risk of illness. Teaching children positive preventive measures, talking with them about their fears, and giving them a sense of some control over their risk of infection can help reduce anxiety. This is also a tremendous opportunity for adults to model for children problem-solving, flexibility, and compassion as we all work through adjusting daily schedules. (National Association of School Psychologists, 2020)

By teaching and modeling soft skills with kids, both teachers and parents can help with the stress and anxiety they have encountered over the last several months. Children are identified more and more as *traumatized, fragile*, and *anxious*. They have more on their plates than in the past and are in need of some answers to help them see a brighter future.

Teachers and administrators deal with misbehavior, lack of motivation, and social issues in schools and classrooms, constantly struggling with how to meet the needs of all children, while teaching an ever-changing curriculum that is required by law. They are looking for answers for how to reach these children, especially those who may be learning online or are academically behind due to loss of in-person schooling.

What can be done to help children learn in a more positive environment, feel safe in the classrooms (either in person or virtually) in which they are placed, and feel valued and respected by those with whom they learn? One possible answer is *soft skills.*

According to Dictionary.com (2018) soft skills are defined as "personal attributes that enable someone to interact effectively and harmoniously with other people." Although working with others is an important part of succeeding in today's classrooms, the idea of soft skills goes beyond just *getting along.* Soft skills are also the skills that students need to reach future goals, remain optimistic, and deal with conflict in their schooling. Soft skills prepare them for future problems, help them to be responsible citizens, and obtain jobs that will empower them in the future.

In the adult world, many books and websites exist about soft skills in the workforce. According to Monster.com (2018), a website that focuses on job skills and careers for adults, soft skills are important in obtaining and keeping a job. "Basically, you can be the best at what you do, but if your soft skills aren't cutting it, you're limiting your chances of career success."

So, if adults are to be prepared and ready for the real world, why not start teaching these skills to children? A recent Senate Bill in the State of Indiana requires the teaching of an *employability skills curriculum* (Indiana Senate Bill 297 2018). This curriculum requires schools to teach the soft skills needed to be successful in future careers such as following directions and arriving on time to work. Although these skills may not be used for years to come, why not start teaching them in a K-12 curriculum?

HARD SKILLS VS. SOFT SKILLS

Soft skills, as outlined above, are the skills that help one get along with others, be prepared for the future with professional behaviors, and have the ability to be flexible and make good decisions. These skills are often hard to measure but are important to the success of one's future career.

Hard skills, on the other hand, are the skills that one learns in a school curriculum. These include the measurable items that are found in a curriculum map or scope and sequence such as being able to comprehend what one reads, having computation skills for math, knowing about how the government operates, and making good decisions for one's health and wellness. They are taught, tested, and evaluated on a daily basis and students receive homework to practice these skills.

Hard skills are also the focus of standardized tests and are measured to determine one's success in school and one's admission to college. Hard skills receive letter grades and impact grade point averages in the lives of students. However, simply knowing the material and passing tests is not enough in today's world.

Being able to communicate with others, be responsible, and work in a team are important characteristics for succeeding in the future as well. Also, being able to have a positive attitude, show composure, and be motivated to do one's best are also vital to accomplishing one's goals. The soft skills of being able to work with others and maintain composure go hand in hand with the hard skills of having the knowledge and ability to do the job well.

As employers look for future job applicants, they need to know who has the hard skills to do the job but also who has the soft skills as well. Knowing that an individual has both sets of skills means that a person is well rounded both in information but in dispositions as well. This book will examine strategies that can be used by both educators and parents to teach the soft skills that are needed to meet the demands of today's world.

The soft skills presented in this book are not a curriculum that is taught a chapter at a time or created in lesson plans. Instead, soft skills are a series of *teachable moments* in which both teachers and parents can witness a problem and teach or model the soft skills that will help kids learn appropriate behaviors, strategies for the future, and ways to help prepare them for college and career readiness. Although it can be read cover to cover, many educators and parents will use the book as a reference guide and teach the soft skills in this book as they are needed by the children in their lives.

Another important belief about soft skills is that this is a book to help teachers and parents work together to help children become well-rounded individuals who are prepared and ready to meet the challenges of the world. It is not about teachers blaming parents, or families blaming educators, it is about working *together* to help kids. An African proverb states, "It takes a village to raise a child" and this is truly what soft skills are about—working together to help raise kids to be their best and to alleviate fears and concerns that they encounter while growing up.

Through collaboration from schools and families, children can learn the soft skills needed for their future at an early age and with activities that are likely already happening at home and in classrooms. Though there are hundreds of soft skills that are needed for a well-rounded child, this book will focus on fourteen of the most important soft skills for children. Each soft skill has an explanation of the components of the skill as well as how teachers and parents can share each skill in the context of experiences and events that are happening in the lives of children. In addition, new information has been added about how to teach soft skills in an online format.

HOW EDUCATORS CAN TEACH SOFT SKILLS

Teachers are an important component in teaching soft skills to children. Since students spend a great deal of time in classrooms, knowing that they have a caring teacher who will provide guidance, influence choices, and teach strategies for success are all important to creating well-rounded individuals.

Educators are key to teaching soft skills as they teach curriculum that encompasses the skills needed for the jobs of tomorrow. They teach the hard skills which include content and technical skills, but they also teach the human skills that will be needed to work with others and be productive citizens in the future.

Modeling by teachers is vital to developing soft skills in children, whether in a classroom or online. Since children are always watching the reaction of their teachers, the way that they handle stress in the classroom, and how they manage time and organization, kids will likely model the behaviors of their teachers in these areas as well. Having teachers who model the soft skills presented in this book will enable children to enter the workforce prepared and ready for the problems and opportunities they will encounter.

Finally, collaboration with parents will help children see that there is a team of caring adults who want to help students make good decisions, learn empathy and respect for others, and have positive outlooks toward their future. By working together with families, teachers can make a huge impact on the future success of children in their classrooms. They can prepare students for the challenges of tomorrow and empower them to be the best they can be. By working together to teach soft skills, the world will be a better place for children.

HOW PARENTS CAN TEACH SOFT SKILLS

Parents are a child's first teachers. They are there from the first day of a child's life to teach and model the appropriate behaviors for children. They share experiences, offer advice, and help children make good decisions and learn from their bad choices. They provide guidance for their families and help them grow and develop into well-rounded individuals.

Families are important in the development of soft skills such as teaching good manners and organization skills. By cultivating these attributes at a young age, parents will be able to help develop children who are respectful and kind to others. They will also show children that soft skills are key to having a successful school experience and in their future world of work and careers.

Parents also model the soft skills contained in this book, whether purposefully or not. Children are always watching their parents to see how they handle difficult situations, make decisions, and handle themselves when things do not go as planned. Children are like sponges and they absorb the characteristics of their parents and the way that they deal with uncertainty and face life's struggles. Knowing that children are modeling a parent's behavior can impact the way that parents react to situations and problems they may encounter.

Finally, collaborating with the school and teacher will enable children to see a partnership of caring adults who want students to be successful in life. By learning about soft skills both at home and in classrooms, children can see that the strategies in this book are important in all areas of a child's world.

HOW TO USE SOFT SKILLS ONLINE AND FOR HOMESCHOOLING

While many parents have been teaching children at home for years through homeschooling and cooperative partnerships, the number of homeschooled children grew drastically during the pandemic of 2020. Whether children were taught at home due to health concerns or because schools were shut down due to the coronavirus, many parents suddenly became teachers. They had to scramble to set up classrooms, gather materials, and in some cases arrange for internet connections and computers for online learning.

Teachers also experienced changes in instruction as they were responsible for hybrid and online learning like never before. They had to learn new software programs, virtual teaching platforms, and how to collaborate with parents and families. Educators had to model a positive attitude while constantly worrying about whether they would have to be quarantined or move to a different teaching format at a day's notice.

Finally, kids had to adapt to ever-changing plans for schools, adapting to learning from home, and always with the threat of an illness in themselves and their families. They missed important events like graduations and proms, and they missed their friends and classmates. Kids had a great deal of anxiety and many questions as their teachers and parents scrambled to make learning happen for them.

When the pandemic occurred, soft skills became an even more important aspect of a child's learning and development. This book was revised and adapted to include not just the original chapters about how teachers and parents could use these soft skills at school and home, but also how to help children learn them in an online environment. The need for each of these skills in online settings was evident and hopefully the new additions will help schools and homes to work more collaboratively in this setting as well.

While learning totally online seemed like a scene from the 1960s cartoon *The Jetsons*, the reality of virtual learning became a reality for most students in the last two years. Hopefully, the new additions about using soft skills in an online environment will help kids adapt to this learning method while also allowing them to develop the skills they need to become well-rounded individuals. The future is bright for students and children. While it may have been a bit rocky lately, kids can be resilient, and persevere through the tough times. As the world returns to normal, the strategy of online learning has proven that it can be done with children and will likely be here to stay. Being prepared for this strategy and armed with soft skills for success in learning are both important for kids to achieve their goals and dreams.

Chapter 1

Communication Skills

Why are communication skills important to kids?
How can educators teach communication skills to students?
How can parents teach communication skills to children?
How can communication skills be taught in an online setting?

IMPORTANCE OF COMMUNICATION SKILLS

Communication skills include being able to effectively speak, listen, read, and write. Communicating means sharing ideas with others, responding respectfully to the ideas of those around us, and being able to correspond with people with whom we work and play. Communication skills start from the birth of a child. When children hear a mother's voice or a father making noises with a toy, they realize that sound represents something.

The first part of communication involves speaking to others. It implies that children have a basic set of oral language skills that enable them to talk and communicate. However, it can also include sign language, braille, and other methods of adaptive communication. Regardless of the method one uses, it implies that people share both words and ideas. Learning to communicate with others is a skill that begins very early in life.

Communication also involves listening skills. Being able to be an effective listener means that one has the skills of eye contact, active listening, and the ability to paraphrase and comprehend what the speaker said. Teaching children to be good listeners implies that the child can interact with others, but also pay attention to information that is being given.

Body language is also included in communication skills for children. According to Dr. Albert Mehrabian (1980), a researcher on nonverbal communication, only 7% of a message is sent through words, 38% through vocal features, and 55% through nonverbal communication such as facial expressions and body language.

1

Teaching a child that one's facial expressions and body language can impact communication is also an important skill to teach children. If a child says that he has done his homework, but has a smirk on his face, parents and teachers will quickly pick up on the body language and know that something is not in place. Body language can also tell friends, families, and others how confident a child is feeling, and how nervous one is. Teaching how to overcome some of these responses can help a child with this skill far into the future.

Communication also includes the use of technology. Learning proper phone etiquette, email manners, and texting protocols will be useful to children. As technology use increases across the world, being able to use a cell phone properly, send an appropriate email to a teacher, or a text to a friend are skills that parents and teachers can teach and refine as children begin using these technologies. Also, teaching children about the impact of cyberbullying and appropriate website usage are important skills for children to learn as well.

Overall, making sure that children know how to effectively speak and listen are key ingredients to raising a well-rounded child who is ready for the future. Making sure that children can communicate respectfully, look a person in the eye, and use a confident voice will be helpful in school presentations, social activities, and even interviews for college and career readiness. The soft skill of communication can be taught and modeled by both teachers and parents and is indeed worthy of the time and energy it takes to teach.

The next section will explain ways that educators can teach communication skills to their children. From teaching the basic curriculum involved in language arts to modeling this skill in the classroom, instructors play a vital part in teaching this skill to children.

HOW CAN EDUCATORS TEACH ABOUT COMMUNICATION SKILLS?

By the time children arrive in school, much of their language skills have already been formed. However, the communication skills that children need to be successful in life can still be modeled and refined in the classroom. At a very early age, teachers can show children how to effectively speak to their friends, use negotiation skills, and solve problems with their peers.

Teaching children to *use their words by asking nicely for a toy, sharing with classmates, and solving problems that happen at recess are great ways to teach a child to stand up for himself or handle a problem that happens with peers. Children need to learn how to compromise and explain how the actions of others can impact them as well. Teaching phrases such as, "When someone takes my toy, I feel sad, and I would like to have it back" puts the words in children's terms and teaches them that communication can be a useful tool when done nicely.*

Helping children to feel comfortable speaking to others in the class is also a skill that teachers of young children can do in the classroom. Allowing children to share thoughts and ideas during community circle or show and tell encourages them to speak in front of others and shows that they have a voice in the classroom. Many teachers also feel that class meetings in the morning help with classroom management and setting a positive tone for the day.

Teaching children about appropriate volume levels is a great way to teach about communication skills in the classroom as well. Some teachers use the idea of an indoor and outdoor voice when teaching this skill, with the idea that an indoor or quieter voice is used in the classroom so that they do not disturb others, and an outdoor voice is used in physical education classes or on the playground where noisy environments are allowed and expected. By teaching about volume levels, educators are preparing children for the etiquette used in an office setting or even a quiet setting such as a church or place of worship.

Reading is another important part of learning communication skills. Teachers must teach the required elements of reading such as phonics, word recognition, and decoding, but also need to teach students to read for information, how to tell if data is from a relevant source, and how to use and interpret what they have read.

Students also need to learn that reading is used for a variety of reasons including using a recipe for cooking, locating facts for an assignment, or simply reading for pleasure. Making sure that real-life applications are taught and used with children can be a great way to make reading meaningful to students, as students who are taught about real-life applications of soft skills will be better able to apply them in their future education and careers.

The skill of listening is another part of communication that teachers can use in the classroom. Doing activities such as reading aloud and having the children recall information, having students listen to directions and perform an activity accordingly, or doing *talk and turns* with a friend or classmate are all ways to teach the skill of listening to children. Many activities are available both commercially and on the internet that focus on listening skills for children. These activities should be intentionally taught to children to further develop listening skills in the classroom.

Writing is a communication skill as well. Teachers can focus on writing and the many purposes of writing that children will need for the future. The simple skill of relating information such as creating a grocery list or writing a note to a grandparent are useful and necessary in today's world. Children who can learn the skill of writing at an early age can realize that this is a powerful tool for communicating and sharing their ideas with others.

Learning to write precise directions for how to do something or communicate through homework activities can also be helpful in teaching writing skills. A wide variety of activities and ways to practice written communication are available to teachers through school curriculum and on the internet. When taught with a real-life application, students will benefit from these skills and be able to use them in their future.

Writing for personal reasons is also a focus of written communication. Whether it is teaching the children to be reflective, consider another person's point of view, or document one's activities through a personal diary, learning to write about one's needs and interests may also be used in the classroom. By using personal reflection, teachers can also get to know the interests of the children in the classroom—a bonus for connecting with one's students.

In brief, there are many ways that teachers can instruct students in the area of communication skills. Although speaking and listening will most likely be used the most in social settings and future job assignments, knowing how to use reading and writing in the real world are also important. By working together with parents, teaching children the soft skill of communication is a must to be successful in today's world. The next section will explain ways that parents can become involved in this process.

HOW CAN PARENTS TEACH ABOUT COMMUNICATION SKILLS?

Parents are a child's first teacher and usually the primary caregiver. Therefore, communication starts from the first day of a child's life. When a baby cries to send the message that she is hungry, needs to have a diaper changed, or is tired, parents learn to interpret and respond to a child's needs. While crying is a very basic communication skill, infants learn at a very young age that this simple action gets attention!

When infants and toddlers begin to develop verbal abilities, parents can help refine and teach these skills with their children. Parents can help identify and teach new words as children are curious and find important things around them. As a child points to a flower at the park, parents can explain and teach the word *flower* in context.

Aside from basic language skills, parents can help children to learn the skills of communication as well. Learning to say thank you for a gift, excuse me when walking in front of others, and a friendly handshake when being introduced to a new person are all skills that parents need to teach and explain to children. Teaching children these skills rather than assuming that they will be taught in school is a huge role that parents can do at home.

According to Arora (2018):

> Possessing a set of proper oral language skills can be described as an essential life skill in today's times. Parents should start teaching their kids basic communication skills during the early years and go on to hone their skills as they grow. Assuming that kids may learn suitable communication skills sans parental guidance can be a huge mistake. Parents may wish to coach their kids not only to communicate effectively but also politely.

While the skill of using manners is explained in depth in a future chapter, knowing how to communicate kindly and professionally is a skill that will be needed in both the school and future work settings. Another skill involved in communication is the use of social cues.

Social cues are noticing and using the appropriate communication skills in the appropriate setting. Parents can teach social cues in several ways. First, parents can teach that certain settings require certain behaviors. For example, a loud voice is used at the park or when playing with one's siblings, while a quiet voice is used at a wedding or funeral. Social cues can also include knowing a child's audience. Talking and being silly with friends may not be the same as speaking to older adults or grandparents.

Looking people in the eye while speaking and standing an appropriate distance from others when talking are also social cues that can be taught and modeled to children. Also, social cues such as how to communicate with someone with disabilities or knowing to use a louder voice when speaking to Grandpa are all social situations that children may need to learn, depending on the circumstances.

The next section will explore ways that communication skills can be taught in an online teaching environment, including children who participate in school through a virtual school setting, those who are learning online due to situations such as pandemic-related education, and others who participate in online learning through homeschooling cooperatives. Regardless of the reason for learning online, communication skills in an online setting are important to kids both now and in the future.

HOW CAN KIDS LEARN COMMUNICATION SKILLS ONLINE?

During the recent pandemic, many children were forced to learn from home, either through a traditional school that moved online, or through cooperative learning pods that used online resources and curriculum. Learning in an online environment created several challenges for both teachers and parents and communication skills were among the most difficult. However, several strategies for communicating in an online format arose including the following.

One important idea for teaching communication skills in an online environment includes educating children on the strategies and etiquette of learning online. Procedures such as knowing when (and how) to mute the microphone in an online environment, how to enable the computer camera, and how to navigate the communication procedures for online learning formats are all important so both teachers and parents can help children learn to communicate in a different format. Taking the time to model these skills to children and train them how to use formats such as Zoom and Google Classroom will indeed be worth the time and effort to help online learning go smoothly.

Creating opportunities for communication in an online environment is also an important skill for teachers of online classes to develop. Considering the age and attention span of the children being taught is important as young children will have a difficult time paying attention if only the teacher is involved in the learning. Creating opportunities for the children to share, work in cooperative groups, and be involved in the learning will help them develop communication skills, even in an online format. Teachers can create breakout rooms where children discuss and solve problems together in smaller, more manageable groups, and can encourage dialogue and discussion in reading and math groups as well.

Another way that educators can teach communication skills is by encouraging all students to participate in the online learning environment. Just like a typical classroom, there will always be some students who are more engaged in the learning than others. Remembering to involve children in the learning, and drawing them into conversations can indeed help keep them attentive and involved in the lesson. Quick polls such as a morning meeting where everyone introduces themselves by telling their favorite ice cream flavor or most interesting hobby are engaging but also allow the teacher to get to know the students while learning virtually.

Parents can also encourage communication skills by arranging other activities that use a virtual format after school hours. Liesl, a kindergartner, created a survey for her friends and relatives, and then made a short video about the results of the survey that she emailed (with her mother's help) to the friends and relatives who participated. By communicating with several people via text and phone to gather the information she needed about their favorite animals, she used communication skills and by creating the video she practiced presentation skills that she will need in school for years to come.

Elaina, a second grader, created a virtual book club for her grandparents. She had her four grandparents read an assigned book and then asked them a variety of questions about it during weekly Zoom conferences. She not only used communication skills in an online setting, but was able to see and talk with her grandparents during a particularly rough time of quarantine. By doing this, she practiced the soft skill of communication, enjoyed time with her relatives, and learned skills that will be important in her future.

Though practicing communication skills in an online environment may take a bit of creativity on the part of both teachers and parents, there are certainly ways to make this happen. Kids need to see that communication is an important part of their lives, regardless of the format. They also need to be taught the skills that accompany learning in an online format and how to use these appropriately—being aware of the safety and dangers of inappropriate uses as well. A conversation about how to use social media safely, guidelines about sharing personal information outside of the school setting, and other important practices should be established both at school and at home.

Overall, learning to communicate effectively is an important soft skill that all children need. From the very beginning stages of infancy, children learn that communicating through crying gets their needs met. However, as they grow and mature, children need to learn that communication is also a way to interact with others and effectively form relationships in both social and professional settings. By learning the skill of communication at school and at home, children can practice this soft skill and be prepared for future encounters with others—whether that be in person or online.

KEY IDEAS

- Communication involves the areas of speaking, listening, reading, and writing.
- While parents may teach beginning verbal skills to children, teachers can refine these skills in the classroom as well.
- Communication skills are needed to effectively participate in school and social activities, but also are needed in the workplace.
- Teaching children about body language and social cues can also be helpful in the area of communication.
- Communication through technology also needs to be taught and modeled to children both at home and school.
- Teaching children communication skills through real-life experiences (both in person and online) is important so that children learn how this impacts them in an authentic way.

Chapter 2

Teamwork

Why is teamwork an important skill to teach kids?
How can educators teach teamwork to students?
How can parents teach teamwork to children?
How can teamwork be taught in an online setting?

IMPORTANCE OF TEAMWORK

Teamwork is an important skill in today's world. People work together on projects, committees, and other endeavors that require collaboration and cooperation. They must learn to communicate, value the opinion of others, and learn to compromise. Teamwork is an important skill in careers of the future and is crucial to teach children at an early age.

By learning to work together, children will develop strategies that will last a lifetime. Parents and teachers who teach the skill of teamwork are allowing students to be able to work with others—a vital attribute in life. According to McQuerrey (2018):

> For students to achieve a comprehensive, well-rounded education, integrated teamwork on several fronts is vital. Teamwork is necessary between students, between students and teachers, and among parents and educators. The more teamwork fundamentals exhibited, the more opportunity exists for students to learn the vital skills of compromise and collaboration.

Teaching about teamwork and collaboration is not always easy to accomplish. Sometimes the people on the team or committee are difficult to work with, and it takes a great deal of effort to do this skill. Learning to listen to the views of others and coming to a compromise takes careful words and actions to accomplish without hurting feelings or saying the wrong thing.

Teaching children the skill of teamwork includes areas such as negotiation, sharing, and active listening in order to be successful. Teamwork is not simply throwing kids in groups, but also teaching them how to work well with others. In real life, conflict occurs, friends have opinions that are different than ours, and people in the office or neighborhood may not always work well together. Children need to learn that working with others is not always easy, but that through the skill of teamwork, tasks will be accomplished, and work can be completed.

By modeling and explaining skills such as cooperative learning, collaboration, and effective communication, both parents and teachers can help students develop the skill of teamwork in children. The following sections will explain ideas for both teachers and parents to help children learn this soft skill.

HOW CAN EDUCATORS TEACH TEAMWORK TO CHILDREN?

Teamwork is a skill that is vital in the educational setting. Students are often called upon to create group projects, do experiments, and participate in activities such as peer editing and math workshops. Being able to work as a team in a learning environment is an important skill that all teachers should model and implement in their classrooms.

Teaching and modeling the skill of teamwork is one that educators can implement from the first moment of class. Showing that the teacher values others and knows how to work appropriately with them is a skill that can be shown in all aspects of the school day. Modeling how one works with school colleagues, parents, students, and others is simple and easy to do. Being kind and respectful of others, promoting a positive learning environment, and displaying the characteristics of a team player can all go far in the classroom setting.

Creating a classroom that works as a team or community is another way to promote and teach the idea of teamwork in the classroom. Referring to the physical environment as our classroom and making the children feel welcome and respected, a teacher can promote the soft skill of teamwork in a very valuable way. If students are included in activities such as creating rules, making decisions, and being responsible for the classroom, they will be more likely to feel like a part of the team environment.

Arranging cooperative learning groups in an intentional manner is also an effective way to teach teamwork in classrooms. Teachers who carefully and strategically select the placement of students in small groups will not only help children learn more effectively but should have improved classroom management as well. By separating certain students from each other, and connecting others for collaboration, the teams will be more successful and the learning more focused. While there are some times when randomly selecting students for group activities such as a quick test review or a fun activity is necessary, taking the time to carefully select which children work together is a strategy that many teachers find helpful.

Another idea for teaching teamwork in the classroom is to identify and teach social skills directly to the students. For example, when a teacher notices that there is conflict in groups or teams in the area of being kind and constructive when offering feedback, the teacher can complete a mini lesson on how to communicate with others in the group, how to say comments in a kind way, and what to do if one disagrees with a group member. By teaching these skills and then watching for them in a group environment, students are more apt to learn the soft skill of teamwork in the classroom setting.

Group projects and team activities are often difficult because of the assessment involved. When teachers grade a project based solely on the product outcome, this can create havoc in the classroom when one student completes all of the work, or when others are slackers (people who do little work and rely on others to do it). By grading both the final product and the cooperation involved, teachers will be able to assess both the project and the social aspect of getting along. This dual assessment can also provide feedback and opportunities for students to grow in the area of teamwork for future lessons.

Friendly competitions in the classroom are also a great way to teach teamwork in the classroom. Often, teachers divide the students into Table Teams or Work Groups to enhance personal and group responsibility. Earning points for showing appropriate behavior, having a clean work area, and being ready to learn are excellent ways to involve students in an elementary setting. For older students, doing review activities, earning points for completing all components of an experiment, and teaching about the value of teamwork in class are all ways to motivate students to be better team players.

Reading novels and stories in which the characters have a problem that they must work together to solve is another way to teach about teamwork in the classroom. Through this bibliotherapy approach children can learn how teamwork is used by reading about it in the lives of others. Students of all ages are capable of empathizing with the characters in the book and identifying the teamwork skills used to resolve conflict or create a solution to a problem. A school or community librarian can assist teachers in finding developmentally appropriate books to reach this goal.

Discovering how others have worked together in the past is also a great way to teach about teamwork in the classroom. Historical figures such as explorers, civil rights leaders, and presidents have had to work together to promote a sense of community, solve problems, and make decisions that will impact others. Discussing the way that teamwork was used in such endeavors will share positive role models and exhibit the importance of teamwork in areas of history as well.

Having students interview adults in their lives about how they use teamwork in their jobs or other activities can explain why this is a vital soft skill for children to learn. By hearing from adults that this is a skill that is practiced in the workplace, faith-based groups, and community organizations, they will see that the teamwork activities taught in classrooms have a purpose for the creation of well-rounded, kind individuals, who know how to work and care for others.

In conclusion, the skill of teamwork is one which children need to be successful in life. Whether they are working with a soccer team to score the next goal, a group of classmates to complete a school project, or an organization to complete a community service project, children need to learn how to work with others, collaborate for a common goal, and be successful in learning the skill of teamwork. Teamwork is a skill which will be needed in all areas of their future lives, both personal and professional. The next section will explain ways that parents can teach this skill as well.

HOW CAN PARENTS TEACH TEAMWORK TO CHILDREN?

Parents can teach teamwork in a variety of ways, from encouraging children to participate in team activities, to explaining ways to work with others. Regardless of the path one chooses, teaching this skill is important for future success.

One of the first ways that children learn teamwork is through organized sports leagues. While these teams are an excellent way to encourage children to work together, they can also be challenging for students as they require effort, patience, and tact in children. Learning to wait one's turn to participate, working together for a common goal, and relying on each other for the good of the team can teach children to the skill of teamwork.

Sports teams can also model teamwork as children see parents and coaches working together as well. Parents who support the team and coaches without placing judgment and yelling at the coaches can model that they support the teamwork that is being formed for the children. Sports leagues can also teach the important skills of being a humble winner and losing with grace and humility, both characteristics that are often lacking in the real world.

Another way to encourage teamwork is through organizations such as scouting, school clubs, and faith-based activities. By working and learning together, children in such organizations can hone the skills of teamwork in activities, community service projects, and other ventures. Working with the same group each week enables children to gain the skills of negotiation, cooperation, and understanding. Not every child is the same and learning to be patient with others and respect their differences in opinions is indeed a skill that all children need.

Teamwork in the family can also be taught by parents. Implementing the team model of parenting, with the idea that the parents are the coaches and the children are all part of the family team, is an innovative way to include children in the teamwork of family. Learning that everyone in the family must work together to respect others, do their share of the housework (including simple chores for young children), and make family-related decisions together can teach children how teamwork is valued—even at home.

While families today are very busy, taking the time to involve children in household decisions such as where to go on the next family vacation, how the family can work together to adopt a new pet, or ways that the family can support an ill relative will make children feel an important part of the family team. It will also help them realize the importance of working together and that this skill is one that can be applied to more than just a sport or school activity.

A final way that families can teach teamwork is by sharing how this skill is used in the adult world. When parents have to work with an unkind co-worker, deal with unruly neighbors, or cooperate with others in a group or organization they can share the options they chose to use, and how teamwork and collaboration skills helped them to compromise and work together. Seeing that teamwork is a life skill that is used by adults on a daily basis will help children learn the importance and use of cooperation later in life.

In brief, learning the skill of teamwork and collaboration is one that can be started in a family setting, long before a child reaches school age. By working together in the home and participating in simple group activities such as sports teams and social groups, children will soon see that working together is an important life skill that they will need in future endeavors.

The next section will concentrate on how to use teamwork in a virtual setting such as how teamwork can be used for school projects, and how the skill of teamwork can be used for outside activities as well. By working together parents and teachers can help students learn this skill through the use of an online environment.

HOW CAN KIDS LEARN TEAMWORK
IN AN ONLINE SETTING?

Although some students participated in teamwork at school through tools such as Google Docs, and creating PowerPoint presentations together prior to the pandemic, much changed when many classrooms moved to an online environment. Teachers were now faced with physical limitations such as not being able to have the whole class in one contained room. Students were now learning from home, and many were separated from their peers and classmates. However, creative teachers developed multiple ways to encourage teamwork even in a virtual setting.

One way to develop the soft skill of teamwork is through breakout rooms in formats such as Zoom and Google Classrooms. By using these tools, teachers were able to create cooperative learning activities that allowed students to create projects and solve problems with smaller groups of children. While it may have taken some creative problem solving on the part of the teacher with concerns such as how to assign groups, how to keep each group on task during discussions, and how to monitor the work of multiple groups in an online setting, teachers were able to come up with a variety of strategies to help with this problem. Doing periodic check-ins with groups, making sure that directions were clear and specific, and providing an appropriate mode for asking questions such as a chat room, teachers are indeed able to build teamwork in an online setting.

Opportunities such as Team Mode in the game-based learning platform of Kahoot! or Microsoft Teams can also help teachers create activities for team building in an online environment. By creating team-based competitions to review skills and practice new information teachers can check on the understanding of their students while also building a classroom community which focuses on teamwork. These friendly competitions also increase the motivation and time on task of the students who are not able to be present in the classroom.

At the high school level, students were able to put together virtual band concerts, plan high school events, and create class projects all during quarantine. The learning of students did not stop when they moved to an online format for school, they just had to think creatively and work harder on the skill of teamwork to communicate effectively and work together from a distance.

Another way that teachers can build teamwork skills is through modeling a strong relationship with parents and families. By clearly communicating expectations with parents, encouraging at home participation, and acknowledging that both parents and teachers need to work together to educate students in an online setting, kids will see that teamwork is a valuable skill—not only in their current education but in their future as well.

Parents can also teach teamwork in an online setting by encouraging their children to work with others in an online environment. Nick, a sixth grader, was unable to attend his Boy Scout Troop meetings due to the pandemic. However, with the help of his parents, he was able to join a virtual Boy Scout Troop and even earned merit badges by completing tasks and projects at home. While it took some extra planning and the preparation of locating materials at home, he was able to participate in team activities, and practice the skill of teamwork, even in a virtual setting.

Learning teamwork by arranging family game nights through Zoom and other conferencing software is also a way that parents can teach the skill of teamwork at home. Grandparents and cousins can be invited to participate in games such as Charades or Hangman in virtual settings and can help alleviate the distance that many families encountered during the recent quarantine.

A final way that parents can help with the skill of teamwork in an online environment is through modeling and sharing their own work with their children. Many families have had to move to working and telecommuting during the recent months. Sharing how this works in the real world, talking about ways that their teamwork skills helped them with virtual office meetings, and sharing about strengths in their own teamwork skills at their jobs and at home will also benefit children in their growth of teamwork skills for the future.

In conclusion, teamwork skills are an important part of learning to work together, both now as students, and also in the future as one prepares for a job which will most likely involve working with others. By learning teamwork skills at school and at home, and being prepared for this skill both in person and in an online environment, kids will be prepared for the future regardless of where their office may be located!

KEY IDEAS

- Being able to work with others is an important soft skill for children and in future workplaces.
- Participating in team sports, group activities, and community service projects is a great way for students to see and use teamwork in the real world.
- Creating a team environment where all classmates work together can help teachers educate students on the idea of teamwork—whether in class or online.
- Carefully selecting groups for cooperative activities and teaching social skills are important ways to teach teamwork in the classroom setting.

- Teamwork skills for home, school, and online platforms are all important for students, as teamwork can be used in all of these areas.
- Modeling the importance of working together by both teachers and families is a great way to show students how teamwork is used to support their education.

Chapter 3

Manners

Why are manners important to teach to kids?
How can educators teach manners to students?
How can parents teach manners to children?
How can manners be taught in an online setting?

IMPORTANCE OF MANNERS

Manners are an important part of daily life. From being greeted in a warm way each morning, to saying please and thank you when receiving gifts, manners can make a child seem well rounded and ready to meet the world. Manners are the way that one behaves around others. They include phrases such as please, thank you, and excuse me, as well as actions such as respect and kindness.

Manners are not something that children are born with. They need to have the soft skill of manners taught and modeled for them by every adult in their lives. They also need to understand when good manners are used, as well as the impact of *bad manners* on others. Seeing how one uses manners on a daily basis is important for children to learn beginning at a very early age.

From the time children learn to speak, they can be coached and expected to say, "Please, thank you, and you're welcome" every time an item is given and received. By having these simple manners as an expectation in homes and classrooms, children will grow up with them as an automatic reaction, and not something done just when company is present. Learning other phrases such as "excuse me" when walking in front of others or when one belches can be added as a child is ready. By learning manners in a developmentally appropriate way, children will acquire a soft skill that will be used for the rest of their lives.

So why are manners so important to children? It is because manners exhibit a well-rounded, kind, and caring person. They show that the child acknowledges the feelings and needs of others and appreciates a helpful deed or kind action. Manners can exemplify a child who shows respect for rules and has learned the proper etiquette to survive in today's world. A child with good manners grows into an adult who is appreciated and respected in the workplace and other social settings.

Teaching children manners at an early age is a soft skill that is also a life-long trait. According to the website The Spruce.com (2019):

> Almost everyone understands that there's a reason for etiquette guidelines and rules for good manners. After all, most parents start teaching polite words and phrases to their children early in life. They know that they're giving their children an advantage that will carry over into social, educational, and eventually professional situations.

By teaching children about manners at an early age, parents and educators are setting the stage for the requirements of being successful in the real world. Although some manners are outright and evident, others may be expected in social settings and in the workplace. By learning the soft skill of manners at an early age, children are apt to be more successful in their adult lives.

So, what is included in the skill of manners and how can educators teach this in the classroom? The following will explain how to do this as well as some ways to model and teach this concept to children.

HOW CAN EDUCATORS TEACH MANNERS?

In the classroom, manners are an important skill to teach and model. Teachers who expect manners and kindness to others in the classroom,create classrooms that are more kind, safe, and have a sense of community. By beginning the school year with the expectation that the classroom is like a family and needs to be a place of kindness, support, and respect, the teacher can promote the idea of manners from day one.

A teacher is also important in the modeling and teaching of manners each day. Young children are very impressionable. If they see a teacher who is respectful and uses good manners, they are more likely to do so as well. At the same time, remembering that all students do not learn this skill in the home is important too. Instead of becoming upset with a child who does not display good manners, taking the time to teach this skill and the importance of it is crucial in its development.

Noticing and praising the good manners and random acts of kindness in the classroom is another way for teachers to enhance this skill in their classrooms. When a child helps an injured child on the playground, or a student who drops their tray in the cafeteria, noticing this kind behavior and saying, "Thank you for helping your friend. That was a very kind thing to do," can go a very long way. Children like to be praised and acknowledged when they exhibit kindness to others, and it is a great way to model the expectations in the classroom.

Acknowledging the work and service of others in the school building is also a way to teach manners in the classroom. A bus driver appreciation card, a thank you to the school secretary, or a note to the school custodian for cleaning the classroom every day are ways to model manners and respect to those who help the children on a daily basis. Students do not often see the work of the other people in a school setting and learning to acknowledge them is a skill that children can take with them into the workplace as they obtain jobs and move to future careers.

Keeping the classroom neat and clean, taking care of school materials, and being respectful of people and their possessions are also important in teaching manners. Because manners are not just words, but actions, learning to respect the property of others and taking the responsibility for the classroom are ways that all children can learn this skill in the classroom. Picking up toys at the end of recess for young children, and cleaning the lab supplies after an experiment for older students are all ways that an instructor can teach about manners through a sense of community in the classroom.

Overall, taking the time to teach and model manners can impact children throughout their entire lives. Many employers notice manners (or the lack of them) in job interviews. An applicant that greets an employer with a warm handshake, looks them in the eye, and uses good manners is one that will stand out in the mix of other interviewees. People who express kindness and use proper manners in an interview are likely to do the same in a work setting—and who would not like to have these people on your team?

HOW CAN PARENTS TEACH MANNERS?

From the time children are able to speak, parents can begin modeling and teaching manners in the home. They can begin with please, thank you, and you're welcome, when someone gives a child a gift, when a server brings the food to the table at a restaurant, and when a friend pays them a compliment. Being aware of this basic step in manners is a great way to start, and makes children seem kinder and more civil, simply with the use of a few basic words and phrases.

Teaching the first few phrases of manners can start simply by modeling with other family members. Parents who thank children for picking up toys, getting an item from the refrigerator, or showing kindness to others will raise children who do the same. Encouraging siblings and even visitors to the home to use these same manners can create an expectation that manners are used and expected in this child's family and home.

Other manners such as opening the door for an elderly person or a parent with a stroller or picking up an item dropped by someone at the library can also be taught and modeled by parents. As children see kindness and behaviors toward others, they are likely to do the same actions when at a store or other public place.

Giving compliments to others is another great way to teach children manners. Learning to give genuine compliments when someone does a nice gesture, a kind deed, or even a mundane task can also model appropriate behaviors toward others. Thanking the mail carrier for delivering the mail, writing a note to the school bus driver at the end of the year, and noticing the services that people do for others is also a way to show appreciation and develop manners in children.

Thank you notes for birthday and holiday gifts are also a wonderful way to teach manners in children. Though this simple act is often forgotten in today's world, it is a great skill for children to learn and one that is appreciated by gift givers and future employers. Having very young children draw a picture of the gift with an adult writing the dictated words of the child is a beginning way to develop this skill. As children get older, having an expectation that thank you notes are written is a way to teach this skill at home. In some homes, the children are not allowed to play with the new toy until the thank you is written—a great way to ensure that this is completed!

In today's world of technology, a text or video are also great ways to make sure that the giver is thanked, without forcing children to write actual notes. A simple text to a grandparent for the birthday money and how it will be used is indeed an effort to thank the parties involved. It may not be as formal as a written note, but it does teach the skill and expectation of acknowledging a gift and the gift giver. It also lets long distance givers know that the gift was received and appreciated.

Another way to thank a gift giver is a quick video of the child opening the gift or playing with the new item. "Thanks for the new book, Aunt Sue" accompanied by the child reading a few pages is a welcome element from a gift giver and allows the person to see the joy in the child using the gift he/she sent. In other words, it is not the actual *note* that makes the difference here. It is acknowledging the gift was received, and that the child appreciates the gift and thoughtfulness involved by the sender.

Aside from the basic ideas of please and thank you, manners can be taught in other ways as well. Picking up one's toys after a play date, helping with dishes after meals, and refraining from texting at the dinner table are also important in teaching good manners. Looking a person in the eye while speaking and offering a hand for a handshake when meeting new people also matter.

In general, simply modeling and teaching the ideas of kindness and respect to others, being responsible for picking up clothes and other possessions, and noticing when someone else shows kindness to others can go a long way in teaching manners to children. While this skill alone could take chapters to write, the important idea here is that manners are embedded in the daily lives of children and are expected in the home and public places.

As Pam Myers (2019), author of "The Importance of Teaching Manners to Kids," stated:

> You do your children such a big favor when you teach them good manners. From bosses to girlfriends, good manners can make or break an opportunity. For instance, if your child is up for his first job and his credentials match another candidate's, the more polite and mannerly candidate may end up with the job.

By teaching and modeling good manners in the home, parents and families will create an environment of respect, and will also teach children the importance of manners in the real world. Taking the time to teach this skill to their children, parents will also find manners to be a rewarding gift that will live forever in their kids.

The next section will concentrate on ways that manners can be taught in an online environment as well. Even though we typically think of manners as being an *in-person* attribute, the way we show manners in a virtual conference or online interaction is just as important in teaching this skill to children.

HOW CAN KIDS LEARN MANNERS IN AN ONLINE SETTING?

Teaching manners in an online platform can be a bit tricky. After all, the people on the other end of the conversation are most likely in another place! While it would be easy to get away with inappropriate manners or unkind behaviors in an online setting, teaching this soft skill to children is just as important as it is when being in the same room with others. Manners are the kindness and respect that one shows to others, such as not interrupting a conversation or thanking people for their contributions. Showing manners in an online setting still matters, as people will remember when one doesn't!

Teachers can model manners in an online classroom by still using and expecting the same manners that they would see in a classroom setting. Remembering to be kind, respectful, and showing appreciation are all still important. Teachers can develop a plan for who speaks during a Zoom conference to eliminate interruptions, and can notice when children are doing a particularly good job of paying attention or contributing to class discussions. Saying thank you and modeling manners for students can go a long way in continuing the use of the good manners we expect in person.

Teachers can also explain the importance of active listening, showing respect, and focusing on conversations in an online environment. Being at home (or in an alternative location) provides much temptation to students, and doing a mini lesson on how the class can practice attentiveness through facial expressions and body language is also important. Eliminating toys or extra items from the learning environment is also a way to show active listening and participation, as they allow students to focus more on the learning at hand. Also, reminding the students that they are still a part of a learning community, even if they are apart, is important in modeling appropriate manners to children.

Parents can also help model good manners in an online format by providing a central place for students to learn, eliminating outside noises like television, and moving younger siblings to a quieter place so that students can learn without interruptions or distractions. This is helpful to both the students and the instructors as it models that the learning and conversations taking place online are important and valued. Of course, the doorbell may still ring, a cell phone may buzz, or a baby may still cry, but attempting to show that online learning is important and valued is a way that parents can model manners through the online learning process.

Remembering to say thank you at the end of a lesson, a class meeting, or a day of learning is another nice way that parents can help with online learning and manners. Approaching a teacher in a kind way when there are issues or concerns, and modeling the importance and value of a child's education are truly helpful in modeling soft skills as well. An online environment is not as personal as an in-person meeting or a parent teacher conference, but a virtual environment can indeed be a place where manners are taught and used. Remembering to show respect and manners to the teacher and working together to solve problems is another way that parents can model appropriate behaviors and show mutual respect to the people involved in the education of their children.

In conclusion, teaching manners to children at an early age will help them be respectful, kind, and noticed. People notice children who act appropriately, use kind manners, and exhibit this skill to others. By working on manners in school, at home, and online, teachers and parents can help raise a generation of children who are polite and kind.

KEY POINTS

- Manners begin with simple words such as please, thank you, and you're welcome.
- Not all children learn manners at home. Being able to teach them in school is important for teachers to do. Working together with parents is even better!
- Manners also include actions such as opening doors for others, cleaning up the toys after a play date, and helping others in need.
- Manners also include items such as sending thank you notes, avoiding texting at the dinner table, and acknowledging the help and assistance of others.
- Manners in an online environment are also important. Even though the students may be in different places, manners are still both valued and appreciated.
- Manners are a soft skill that is noticed by others and can help in social skills, educational endeavors, and even future job settings.

Chapter 4

Respect

Why is respect an important skill to teach kids?
How can educators teach the skill of respect to students?
How can parents teach the skill of respect to children?
How can respect be taught in an online setting?

IMPORTANCE OF RESPECT

Respect can be a difficult concept to explain to children. It is a term that adults frequently use, but often do not take the time to define in words that children can identify with. However, defining this term in simple, child-friendly terms is an important start to teaching this soft skill to children. According to Talking Tree Books (2019), "Respect is a big concept to grasp. Try this definition of respect for kids, written in terms children can understand, and with examples of what is respect for others and what is respect for self. A definition of respect includes 1) how you feel about someone and 2) how you treat him/her."

Learning to respect oneself and others is a characteristic that is often defined by actions rather than words. Children learn the soft skill of respect by watching adults in their everyday interactions and how they treat others. Respect is showing kindness to others when helping an elderly person or treating someone in a thoughtful way when there is conflict. Children learn respect when they see how their parents handle stressful situations or show compassion to someone that they encounter.

Respect is a way of life in many households and classrooms, when children treat each other with care and concern. They show empathy when they see others with problems or concerns and are caring, kind, and helpful. It is also seen when children do compassionate deeds and show actions that are thoughtful of others. Respect is also apparent through the use of good manners and proper actions.

Respect is also seen in children who practice the skill of self-respect. Self-respect, according to Cambridge Dictionary.com, is 1. a feeling of respect for yourself that shows that you value yourself: 2. positive thoughts and feelings about yourself; self-esteem (Cambridge Dictionary 2019). Children who have respect for themselves and think positively about themselves are apt to show more respect to others.

The famous saying by author Leo Buscaglia, "To love others you must first love yourself," is very true in teaching the concept of respect to children. (Buscaglia n.d.). If children are not taught the idea of self-respect and valuing self, it will be very difficult to practice the skill of respect with others. One must start with pride and satisfaction with one's self in order to show the skill of love and caring for others. Working on self-esteem and self-care are both great ways that adults can begin teaching this skill to children.

Teaching self-respect involves teaching children to have pride in their work, taking care of their possessions, and having an attitude of caring and concern about their overall well-being. Teaching children to be humble, gracious, and genuine when they do well are also included in this skill. Being able to be both a winner and a loser without bragging, boasting, and saying hurtful things shows not only self-respect, but respect to others as well.

Taking care of one's health, cleanliness, and hygiene are also important keys to self-respect. Taking care of one's possessions, being clean and healthy, and promoting a lifestyle of healthy habits are other important skills in learning to value self in children. Avoiding negative people and unhealthy habits, taking care of one's property, and practicing self-respect on a daily basis are the keys to learning to respect others.

By first learning the skill of self-respect, children will be ready to respect others as well. Respecting others is a skill that both teachers and parents can teach to children in their care. By showing concern and caring for the well-being of children, allowing them to have ownership and decision-making opportunities, and modeling respect for others, they can show children that the skill of respect is an important one. The next section will explain ways that teachers can enhance this skill in the classroom.

HOW CAN EDUCATORS TEACH RESPECT TO CHILDREN?

Teachers help children learn the soft skill of respect in schools and classrooms. Many teachers begin the school year with teaching students about rules and procedures, several of which involve the idea of respect in some way. Modeling skills such as taking turns and sharing toys shows even the youngest children how to implement this skill in the classroom.

Beginning the school year with activities that promote both self-esteem and respect to others are ways that teachers can promote this skill in the classroom. Teaching children to take care of themselves and their property are important items to consider when working with a new class of students. Talking about what it means to have self-respect and show kindness to others in the form of good deeds, a caring environment, and a considerate classroom are all strategies that are easy to teach and helpful to all.

Having class mottos and expectations of treating others with respect or *respecting self, people, and property* are all simple ways that teachers can explain and teach this disposition in the school setting. Creating a sense of community in the classroom and teaching children the importance of caring will help develop a kind and compassionate classroom of students.

Reading books about characters who are kind, respectful, and make good decisions is another way that teachers can promote respect in the classroom. Discussing the actions of the characters and how these actions impacted others will model the idea of respect through reading and applying this skill to real-life situations. Students who are surrounded with good role models—both real and fictional—will learn about appropriate behaviors and the importance of treating others with kindness and respect.

Taking care of issues such as teasing and bullying in a swift manner is also a way that teachers can instill respect in their students. Instead of ignoring problems such as arguments between children, unkind words, or other unpleasant situations, teachers who turn these events into teachable moments will be able to explain, model, and instruct students about how to better handle such situations in the future. Asking children how they would feel if the tables were turned can help them empathize with the other student and learn to think about their actions before doing them.

Class meetings that deal with disrespectful situations or altercations in the classroom are a way for teachers to deal with problems that can occur. Having a class meeting in which the children are allowed to voice opinions, listen to others, and brainstorm possible solutions helps model a respectful classroom where others are valued and respected. By allowing students ownership and rights in the classroom, a teacher models the respect he/she has for the students and develops a sense of family and community among the children.

Older students can be shown respect in the classroom as they earn more rights and privileges when they show maturity and responsibility in the classroom. By noticing the proper behaviors and actions of students, a teacher can reward such behavior by allowing the students a bit more freedom and autonomy than they once had. Older students appreciate and acknowledge when teachers are respectful of them and will return this respect in time.

Supporting the strengths and talents of individual students will also help teachers enhance the skill of self-respect in the classroom. Teachers who concentrate on the talents of children and assist them in strengthening the skills they are lacking will help them to see that they are important and valuable to others. By developing the skill of self-respect, teachers can help them learn to respect others as well.

Activities which promote the abilities and talents of children and are differentiated to meet their needs are strategies that teachers can use to promote both self-respect and respect for others in the classroom. Learning that all children are different and allowing students to explore interest areas, hobbies, and areas of strength are all ways that teachers can enhance the self-esteem in children, while also promoting the respect of different abilities, values, and cultures as well.

By allowing children to concentrate on their strengths, collaborate with others, and truly learn to value the abilities and differences of others, teachers can help both individual students and the classroom as a whole. Learning to respect classmates and working together on both areas of strength and deficits can promote an admirable learning environment where children learn to love themselves and appreciate others with whom they learn.

Encouraging children to interact with children who have disabilities and creating an atmosphere of acceptance is another key to learning respect in the classroom. With the creation of inclusionary classrooms, students are more apt to accept and learn about the needs of others and learn to respect them—both in and out of school. Working with children in a classroom setting means that teachers can set the tone for a loving, caring environment of learning in which *all* children are accepted and taught in respectful ways.

In brief, educators play an important role in the development of respect in children. Teachers who are respectful of children, model and teach kindness, and encourage their students to show compassion and empathy will create classrooms which are community-oriented and places where children can grow. Educators who teach the skill of self-respect will mold children into adults who are well balanced and accepting of others. By working together with parents, teachers can accommodate children, model appropriate behaviors, and develop a skill that will last a lifetime.

HOW CAN PARENTS TEACH RESPECT TO CHILDREN?

Parents can begin teaching the soft skill of respect to children by first modeling this skill in the home. Parents who are kind and loving to each other and the other members of a family are truly the first ways that children see this behavior modeled for them. Showing caring behaviors and expecting this from all members of the household is a great beginning. Even though parents and siblings might disagree with each other, they can still be taught to demonstrate the characteristics of respect. Families argue, disagree, and even fight on occasion, however, learning how to handle these disagreements in a respectful manner is key to the development of this skill in children.

Modeling and teaching kindness and respect to others is also a way that parents can teach this skill to children. Demonstrating kindness and manners to others through actions such as opening doors, saying "excuse me," and extending a hand to those in need are all simple but valuable ways to do this.

Helping a stranger who drops their groceries in a store, assisting a neighbor with raking the leaves, or taking dinner to an ill friend are all respectful actions and can teach about caring and concern for others. Treating others (even strangers) with respect shows children that exhibiting kindness and caring are skills that take very little effort but can make others feel loved and appreciated. Also, helping others often makes us have a positive feeling— simply because seeing another person smile and be thankful for our help just makes us feel good.

Respect can also be taught by parents when their children see them in stressful situations. How a parent handles himself in situations like a traffic jam, with a disrespectful person at the grocery store, or an unruly neighbor are all ways that children can witness the skill of respect in the family. When parents react with anger, or with inappropriate words and actions, children will see this, and often mimic the same actions in later situations. However, if parents can model such circumstances with grace and dignity, children can learn that respect can help de-escalate situations as well.

We all make mistakes. Even the server who brings the wrong food, the person who doesn't use a turn signal while driving, and the clerk who rings up the wrong item are all worthy of forgiveness. Modeling kindness and respect are ways that children watch parents display this behavior. Instead of cussing and swearing, or being unkind and threatening, parents can kindly ask for a new item, explain a problem in a calm way, and in turn model respect—even in stressful situations.

Parents can also model and teach respect by displaying this skill to others. Many years ago, children were taught to respect elders and to respect authority figures. However, this is not always modeled in today's homes. Teaching children to respect their teachers, coaches, and authority figures such as police officers is an important part of teaching respect to others. Even when parents disagree with these people, it is key to take care of problems or concerns in a respectful and kind manner. Children are watching how parents handle certain issues, and not putting children in the middle of such actions is important for parents to remember.

Remembering that respect is *earned*—and not an automatic action—is the vital component of this skill. Parents who model kindness and compassion to others will raise children who use respect in their homes and in other venues.

At the same time, parents who model unkind words and actions will raise children who use these actions as well.

Finally, promoting the skill of self-respect is important in the home. Parents need to teach children to have positive thoughts, and to love and accept themselves as they are. Having realistic expectations, teaching children to be humble, and helping children to have a balance between bragging and being proud are all components of this skill. All children have bad days, bring home a poor test grade, or go through phases where they don't love their appearance, but teaching children to appreciate who they are and accept those bad days in life will help teach about self-respect.

Children also have great days when they bring home a good report card, hit a home run, or perform a dance in the school play. Praising children and showing pride in them are ways that parents can help with self-esteem, but allowing children to brag or boast too much can hinder the development of self-respect in children. Teaching an appropriate level of self-respect that is positive without being unkind is a way that parents can help with this skill. Since self-respect is the basis for learning to respect others, learning this skill at an early age is vital to the development of children.

Overall, the skill of respect is one that is first modeled and taught in the home. Having families that exhibit respect in the household by helping others, being positive, and showing empathy will produce children who are kind to others including classmates and future co-workers. Being respectful is a characteristic that is noticed by teachers, employers, and others. When one is treated with respect and kindness, it is remembered by all.

The next section will explain ways to teach the soft skill of respect in an online setting. With more and more classes and schools using an online environment for teaching and learning, this skill will become increasingly important for children to learn.

HOW CAN KIDS LEARN RESPECT ONLINE?

While respect seems like a skill that is most often practiced with face-to-face interaction, respect can be taught and practiced online as well. During the coronavirus pandemic, many schools were moved to online learning and parents suddenly became teachers overnight! Being respectful of all parties involved can be a great start to practicing this skill, as teachers never planned to teach in a format that broadcast their teaching to homes, and parents never planned to have cameras looking into their households on a daily basis!

Setting up a learning environment that is distraction free, has few interruptions, and is professional are all important. Everyone remembers the online student who took his computer with him to use the restroom and the reporter who participated in an interview without wearing pants! Remembering to explain this to students is a great way to set the tone for teaching respect in an online setting. Teachers can also create online learning environments, even if they are teaching from home. Having an "office" or classroom set up for teaching is much more appropriate than teaching from one's kitchen table!

Teachers can also promote respect in an online environment by encouraging taking turns, having students raise hands to speak during discussions (or using the hands up emoji available in some discussion formats), and encouraging students to mute themselves during whole class discussions. One of the most difficult parts of teaching an online discussion is managing this very important part of online teaching. In a typical classroom, a teacher can use proximity and *the teacher look* to manage his/her group of students. Without these two important strategies, an educator needs to take the time to truly teach and develop this skill with children in order to deliver lessons without interruptions.

Finally, teachers and parents can work together to develop respect in online learning in all age groups. For younger students, parents can sit down with their children (with the assistance of the teacher) to help navigate the online learning during the first few days of class. With older students they can monitor class attendance and behaviors by checking in occasionally to make sure students are being on task and respectful. Both teachers and parents can also model respect when problems such as lost internet connections or unclear communication occur. By remembering that everyone is doing their best to help students learn (even when the internet goes down), students will see this important skill modeled by the adults in their lives as well.

In brief, by working together to help children understand the parameters of online learning, such as when to speak, how to prepare a learning environment, and working to avoid distractions, both teachers and parents can model for children how to be kind and respectful even in an online environment. The learning may be a bit different than a typical classroom, but by practicing respect and allowing a bit of grace, an online learning format can indeed help children practice this soft skill in their education.

KEY IDEAS

- Respect is the way that one thinks about others and how one treats them.
- Teachers can model the skill of respect to children by showing compassion and kindness as well as how they treat others in stressful situations.
- Respect is earned. The more one respects others the more one is respected. This is a skill that is noticed and appreciated by others in school and in future job settings.

- Teaching self-respect is also an important skill for children to learn.
- Parents can also teach and model respect at home by showing kindness and caring to others.
- Both parents and teachers can help children learn respect in an online learning environment by working together.

Chapter 5

Empathy

Why is empathy an important skill for kids?
How can educators teach this skill to students?
How can parents teach the skill of empathy to children?
How can empathy be taught in an online environment?

IMPORTANCE OF EMPATHY

Empathy is an important soft skill for children to learn, both at home and at school. Learning to think how others think and how one's feelings impact their decisions can help children develop this soft skill in their early years. According to Lawrence Kutner, author of "How Children Develop Empathy":

> To empathize with someone is to understand what he is feeling or, more properly, to understand what you would feel like if you were in his situation. It is an extension of self-concept, but it is far more complex. It requires an awareness that others think of themselves in ways that are both similar to and different from the way you do, and that they also have emotions they associate with those thoughts and images.

Empathy in children can be a tricky skill to teach. It is not something one learns in a parenting class or in a college course. It is a spur of the moment skill that children cultivate over time as they witness the emotions of others and try to imagine how they are feeling at that moment. Empathy is a developmental skill that takes time and maturity to learn. A kindergarten student will not have the same depth of empathy as a high school senior.

Children learn empathy when problems occur, a friend gets hurt, or a happy event takes place. They learn to put themselves into the situation to try to see how the other person feels and why their reactions match those feelings. They also learn empathy when others are kind and caring as well. When a friend helps after a fall on the playground or a classmate offers a listening ear in a high school class, students learn that empathy is a skill that will make them better people.

Media and social media are also ways that model compassion, or even poor decisions made by people in the news. Children see both caring acts and unkind deeds happen in the wake of media outlets. They often question why bad things happen to good people and want to know why individuals make the decisions that they do. However, instead of dismissing an awkward question at the dinner table or classroom meeting, adults can take these opportunities to teach the skill of empathy and help children learn how people feel in these situations.

Empathy is also an important life skill which can take one far in a future career. People who are well rounded in the area of empathy work well with others, in school and in the work force. Knowing how others feel and putting oneself in their place will enable people to be more kind and caring as life happens around them. Teaching this soft skill to children will help them learn as children and will enable them to be well rounded adults in the future. The following section will explain how teachers can help teach this skill to children.

HOW CAN EDUCATORS TEACH EMPATHY TO CHILDREN?

Teachers play an important role in developing empathy in children. They are in classrooms on a daily basis and can teach and explain situations in which empathy matters. How a teacher reacts to a child who is ill, a child whose feelings are hurt, or a student who is dealing with a difficult home life can impact how students in the classroom react to these events. Children know when someone in the classroom is struggling. Watching the teacher handle these situations can model the soft skill of empathy.

Using the phrase of "How would you feel if that happened to you?" is also a beneficial skill to use in the classroom. Children often make spontaneous decisions without thinking about how this will impact others. Simply reversing the roles and asking about feelings and actions of others can be a great way to teach this skill to children.

Every day in classrooms across the world, teachers encounter situations in which children get hurt, make poor choices, and see unkind deeds. It is not because children are innately *bad*, it is simply because they do not know how to handle such situations in an adult way. Taking the time to explain how one's actions impact others and how one would feel in the same situation is a great way to teachers to develop empathy in their classrooms.

Asking about the feelings of others is also a skill that can be used in the content one is teaching. When reading about a character who is treated unkindly, asking how the children would feel in this same situation is a skillful way to teach empathy in the content that is already required.

Using this same approach with people in history who were treated unfairly is also a tool for teaching empathy. Many people in the history of the world were not treated with kind words or had bad things happen to them. Allowing students to focus on the reactions of others and how they were treated can introduce empathy with real characters and actions.

Completing service opportunities such as volunteering or collecting items for others is another great way to teach empathy in the classroom. Volunteering to help with younger children at the school or collecting items for a local food pantry can enable students to learn the needs of others and create compassionate people as a result. By putting others first and considering their feelings, students will see that even children can make a difference.

Learning about community needs, advocating for the environment, and helping with social justice causes can help children learn empathy in the classroom as well. Talking about how throwing trash on the ground, or adding pollution to the water helps children learn their impact on poor choices and advocating for a cause can allow children to empathize with others. As long as a teacher has administrative permission for any controversial ideas, this too will help children perfect the soft skill of empathy.

In all, empathy is an important soft skill for children of all ages. By learning empathy, they will be able to put themselves in another person's place, explain how others may feel in similar situations, and hopefully learn to be caring and compassionate as a result. Children learn empathy through the relationships they have with others and parents and educators play a major role in this learning.

Children who learn empathy at an early age are apt to be more kind and caring with others in their schools and social activities. However, one of the most important keys to this soft skill is that teaching empathy to students will allow them to carry this behavior into the adult world of college, careers, and civic engagement. Empathetic children become caring co-workers and kind employees when they reach adulthood, and that will make the world a better place!

HOW CAN PARENTS TEACH EMPATHY TO CHILDREN?

Empathy is not a skill that children are born with. They learn it through watching others, being in certain situations and seeing how people handle real-life situations. As Lawrence Kutner, author of "How Children Develop Empathy," put it:

> Unlike intelligence and physical attractiveness, which depend largely on genet-
> ics, empathy is a skill that children learn. Its value is multifold. Children who
> are empathic tend to do better in school, in social situations, and in their adult
> careers. Children and teenagers who have the greatest amount of skill at empa-
> thy are viewed as leaders by their peers. The best teachers of that skill are the
> children's parents.

Empathy is often learned by watching one's parents handle difficult situations and how they deal with the feelings of others. It is a soft skill that children develop over time and families are probably one of the most influential aspects of how this skill is learned. Children watch their parents and model their empathy after them. Teaching this skill to one's children can happen in many ways.

First, empathy is developed when one witnesses acts of caring and com-passion. Watching a parent help a friend in need, having an adult who does caring deeds, and talking with them about why they made the choices they did can enable a child to become more empathetic. When a friend is ill and a parent makes dinner or runs errands to help, they are modeling empathy and compassion to their children. When a co-worker gets behind on a project and a parent offers to help so that she can attend her child's ball game, children see empathy happening before them.

By modeling and encouraging compassionate acts, children can see how kindness can help others. When a friend loses a grandparent, a child can make a card and simply learn that the words "I'm sorry" can go a very long way. Teaching children that empathy can be shown in one's words and actions is a key skill for children to learn for the future.

Working with people who have disabilities, volunteering to help collect items for hurricane victims, and helping an elderly neighbor with her garden-ing are also ways that parents can teach and encourage empathy. Even young children can help with these efforts, alongside their parents and siblings. By doing so, little ones can learn the importance of empathy and compassion with people who are in need.

Media and social media are also prevalent in a today's homes. Watching the television in the evening with the family, a child can learn empathy by discussing how a character must have felt in a movie or television program. Also, monitoring social media and being aware of situations where cyberbul-lying has taken place are opportunities for teenagers to discuss these prob-lems with their parents. Allowing teenagers to voice their opinions and come up with better solutions will enable them to practice the skill of empathy through teachable moments in the household.

Reading books to children at bedtime is an event that happens in many households. It is calming and allows a parent to build relationships with his/her children while doing so. However, it can also be used as an opportunity to develop empathy as well. Stopping during the story to ask how the character feels and what the child would do in that situation can build empathy with very little effort. It simply takes a few minutes of time and some careful thought to ask the questions that will help guide children in this area.

By modeling and teaching empathy to children, parents can create children who are understanding, compassionate, and caring. Kids look up to the adults in their lives and parents are the first people to show them how empathy works. They model how to help other people in difficult situations and answer questions about challenging topics. Teaching empathy is one that often comes about during sad or unhappy times, and teaching and modeling how to handle these times for children is indeed important for parents to do in the home.

The next section will explain ways that one can teach the soft skill of empathy in an online environment. Even though students and teachers may not physically be in the same location, this skill is an important one to learn, regardless of the place where the learning occurs.

HOW CAN KIDS LEARN EMPATHY IN AN ONLINE SETTING?

As defined in the beginning of this chapter, empathy is understanding what someone is feeling and knowing how you would feel in a similar situation. Doing this in an online setting can be a bit more difficult than in a face-to-face environment, but it is indeed still possible. Even though kids may not be in the same room as the others they are learning with, teachers and parents can still provide for this skill in an online setting.

In a recent observation of an online lesson with first graders, a child told the teacher that his dog had passed away the night before. In a classroom setting, the teacher could have shown a sad facial expression, said some words of condolence, and given this child a hug. However, in an online setting empathy is a bit harder to show and express. Instead, the teacher still took a moment to recognize the child, said that she knew this made the young man very sad, and said that she was very sorry to hear about his loss. By taking a few moments to empathize with this student about his dog, the teacher showed caring and concern, even though she could not physically be with him.

Empathy can also be shown online when a teacher takes the time to develop relationships with students by asking how they feel or what concerns them about the online learning or other issues in general. Since teachers cannot observe the body language and facial expressions of their students quite as well in an online environment, they can take the time to have morning meetings to discuss such issues. In the beginning of an online learning process a teacher can conduct a morning meeting where students share their thoughts and concerns about learning online versus in person. Young children can share their concerns about not seeing their friends at school and high school students can share their anxiety about an upcoming research project. As the group begins to develop an online relationship and get to know each other, the teacher can also provide morning meetings about other concerns and problems that the students may be dealing with. Taking the time to have a meeting which starts with, "I've noticed that this week you seem more tired and less motivated than usual. How can I help?" can go a very long way to sharing concerns and developing empathy.

Parents can also help teach and model empathy at home. During the pandemic, many parents were unexpectedly working from home and doing their tasks in an online environment as well. Sharing how this impacted them, how they communicated with co-workers and completed projects, and how they felt about working online can help children see that they are not alone in their feelings. Parents can share that they also missed their friends and co-workers, or that they felt a little more nervous doing a presentation via Zoom. By doing so, parents can empathize with their students about missing classmates and doing things a bit differently than normal. Modeling empathy and sharing personal stories about similar situations are both ways that parents can help their children learn empathy in an online environment.

A final way that empathy can be taught is by talking about the needs of others, even if we cannot physically see them. During the pandemic, many grandparents did not see or visit grandchildren for very long periods of time. Talking about ways to show caring and concern for them by doing online video conferences, coloring a special picture, or even writing a personal note or letter can help children show concern and kindness from very far distances. Schools that shared virtual events such as awards ceremonies and graduations with relatives who were unable to attend were also excellent ways to share joy and positivity in an online setting.

Even though we typically think of empathy as a soft skill that is taught in person by picking up on joy and sadness in a person's voice and body language, empathy can still be taught in an online environment as well. By practicing careful listening, and taking the time to address students' concerns and problems, both teachers and students can show empathy. Discussing ways that adults learn and communicate in an online platform as well as the concerns and problems associated with this can also help children develop empathy. Finally, encouraging children to do kind things and share successes with others in an online format can help others participate in meaningful and important activities and events that they may have normally missed. Learning empathy will be beneficial to children as they enter the real world of work and society. A kind and empathetic co-worker is something every future employee would like to see in the workplace.

KEY IDEAS

- Empathy is a skill that children are not born with. It is a skill that they learn and develop over time.
- Children learn empathy through watching others. They watch the parents and teachers in their lives, and model their behaviors.
- Difficult situations are often times where students learn the most empathy. Taking the time to discuss these with children is important.
- Volunteering, helping others in times of need, and doing kind deeds can help even young children learn the skill of empathy.
- Children develop empathy in all settings, including classrooms, homes, and online environments. Realizing that empathy can be taught in any situation is an important part of this soft skill.
- By teaching and modeling empathy in children, parents and teachers create adults who will go far in their future careers.

Chapter 6

Composure

Why is composure important to kids?
How can educators teach composure to students?
How can parents teach the skill of composure to children?
How can kids learn the skill of composure in an online setting?

IMPORTANCE OF COMPOSURE

Composure, according to a recent edition of *Psychology Today,* is "the ability to remain calm yet focused under pressure" (Nemko 2018). When someone gets upset by the actions of others, a problem at home, or a situation at school, they are apt to become angry; it is human nature. However, it is how one handles that anger that is important. Becoming angry but being able to remain calm and focused is the key to composure.

We see composure around us every day. The gymnast who takes the floor in the Olympics and never looks nervous is showing composure. A father in the grocery store who has three screaming children, yet remains calm, cool, and collected is modeling composure. The teacher who sees a child injured on the playground, yet calmly handles the situation shows composure as well.

Getting angry is a part of growing up. Kids see or hear things that make them upset. They get into arguments with siblings and have disagreements on the playground. However, being able to handle this anger in an appropriate way is the key to learning composure. A composed child works out problems rather than holds grudges. A composed child uses problem solving instead of yelling unkind words, and a composed child learns a sense of compassion and kindness in dealing with problem situations.

Composure is also learning to deal with emotions and outbursts in an appropriate way. Rather than throwing a fit or tantrum when another child will not share her toys, a composed child will ask kindly and learn to take turns. A child who exhibits composure will also be able to use self-soothing techniques that will be able to de-escalate the anger to a minimal level. Being able to count to ten for example, can teach a child to step back, examine the problem, and not act hastily.

Composure is a soft skill that is needed both at home and school. At home, children must interact with others in the family, including parents, siblings, and even the family pets. When a child interacts with others on a daily basis, tension is bound to happen. Simply living in the same environment, day in day out, with the same people makes that friction occur. However, learning how to deal with this tension can help children learn composure at home.

Conflict also occurs at school, whether that conflict occurs with others or internally. Children may have disagreements, arguments, and conflict with peers over projects, group structures, and viewpoints. They may also have internal conflict when they struggle with the course material, forget to complete homework, or are just having a bad day. Learning ways to remain calm, focused, and relaxed in the midst of such conflict is the key to composure.

The following sections will explain ways that both teachers and parents can model the soft skill of composure. Learning this skill will help in all areas of life, whether it is in a sporting event, a speech one must make for school, or in the work setting when presenting a proposal to one's boss. Composure is a tool that is needed in life, and a skill that will be used in childhood and beyond.

HOW CAN EDUCATORS TEACH COMPOSURE TO CHILDREN?

Educators can begin by modeling the skill of composure to children. When a schedule changes, a child misbehaves, or the computer stops working, teachers need to model a calm and collected attitude to children. According to author and educator Annette Breaux:

> It's not our feelings that determine who we are to others, but rather our actions. And one of the most difficult tasks to accomplish as a teacher is the ability to control your actions and maintain your composure at all costs. (Breaux 2019)

A teacher who remains calm in the middle of a confrontation, speaks kindly to an upset parent, and deals with problems appropriately is one that models composure to children in his/her classroom. A teacher who can take a school situation such as a weather delay or school intruder drill and remain calm and composed will model both a calm and safe environment to children. Focusing on remaining calm models for students that they are safe and that the adults are in control of such situations. The ability to do this is an asset to both a school and the students.

Talking about people who have faced problems or adversity both in history and the present can help students understand the skill of composure as well. A historical figure who had to make difficult decisions, rely on others, and use decision-making skills can be shared as an example of a person who showed composure even under fire. A character in a book can also become the focus of a group discussion when she faces bullying or another stressful situation. Equipping students with the knowledge of how others overcame problems or handled stressful situations are excellent ways for making this skill more realistic to children.

Working with the school counselor, school nurse, parents, and others is also beneficial in helping children learn composure. A school counselor can help children who are overly sensitive or worry about problems more than they should. A school nurse can teach about the physical effects of stress on the body, and parents can help work alongside teachers if a child has extreme issues such as panic attacks or tantrums. Working together with all parties involved in a child's life represents a community of people who want to help children remain safe and learn to be less stressed and focused.

Teaching self-soothing skills with early learners, and stress management techniques with older students is another way that teachers can successfully teach composure in the classroom. Taking a brain break when the classroom instruction gets overwhelming, teaching children to take deep breaths and focus on their learning, and teaching problem-solving skills to students are also valuable. If a child can learn to take care of himself and manage stress, he will be more likely to handle high-pressure situations and will be more ready for the real-life stressors he may encounter.

Composure is a skill that is needed by both children and adults. It is about how one handles the stressors in life that can make a difference in how one handles problems and adversity in the future. By learning to be composed as children, students will learn to use this skill in their college studies and future careers as well. The next section will explain how parents can teach this skill at home.

HOW CAN PARENTS TEACH COMPOSURE TO CHILDREN?

The first way that parents can teach composure in the home is by modeling it. Accidents happen, stressful things take place, and everyday problems ensue. Milk gets spilled, traffic gets backed up, and things get broken. However, it is how parents handle problems like the spilled drink, the traffic jam, or the broken item that is viewed by the children who are watching.

A parent who takes control of the situation by cleaning up the spill or broken glass swiftly but without losing her cool is the parent that is modeling composure for her children. The father who takes the traffic jam or broken lawnmower in stride is also modeling composure. However, a parent who yells, swears, and loses control not only does actions without thinking, but also models these actions to children. According to Pam Nicholson (2019), author of "Staying Calm During the Storm":

> When parents model assertiveness and calmness, children can learn how to manage their own angry feelings in a constructive and effective way. With an attitude of acceptance toward the inevitability of anger, with some techniques in mind, and with conscious effort on your part to stay cool, you can help your children learn to manage, in a healthy way, the anger that is an expected and normal part of the human experience.

Anger is a common human emotion. Everyone has events or problems that make them angry. However, by learning the skill of composure, children will learn how to deal with this appropriately in order to remain calm and focused.

Stress and anxiety are also areas where composure is needed to be successful. Dancing in a recital, participating in a competition, or playing in sporting events are fun, but often nerve-wracking events. It is great to be the lead dancer in the school performance, but it is also a stressful situation. Competing in a school debate is interesting but can also cause anxiety. Throwing the game-winning free throw is exciting but is also a daunting task. Teaching children how to practice calmness and staying focused can help them be successful without falling prey to nerves.

Practicing both the skills involved, such as the dance moves needed and free throws in the backyard, can certainly help a child be prepared for competitive situations, but also teaching the skills of being a humble winner and graceful loser are also important components in teaching composure to children. When children win a game or competition, for example, remembering to not become boastful and condescending to others is important. At the same time, learning to be a graceful loser is important as well. We can't all win every game. However, by learning these skills we will learn the appropriate ways to both win and lose in the future.

Teaching children relaxation techniques such as deep breathing, counting to ten, and focusing on the task at hand can also help children learn the skill of composure. Reminding children to schedule time for fun and relaxation is also helpful. While dance and debate may be great skills to learn, children also need to be encouraged to relax and *put their feet up as* well.

Hearing an adult's examples about a past problem which was difficult to manage can also help children learn about composure. Learning about the ways an adult handled such issues can help children form their own coping strategies. By helping them understand that everyone has problems and stressful situations in their lives, children can see that composure is a soft skill that is needed and used in their everyday lives.

Responding to children's temper tantrums and anger in an appropriate way is another way to help teach and model composure in the home and in public. If a child throws a fit in a public place, either ignoring the behavior, or talking in a calm, quiet manner can help the situation. Parents who scream and lose control of their own emotions will model this behavior to children and will likely raise children who mimic the same behaviors in the future.

Using the term *composure* and pointing out examples of it are also great ways to teach this skill in the home. When the athlete on television is about to take the game winning putt, pointing this out to children and talking about ways that the person uses composure to breathe, concentrate, and focus is a useful life skill. Seeing a character in a movie who is under pressure can create a productive conversation about how they remained calm even in the midst of adversity.

By teaching about composure and how to handles times of stress, parents can assist their children in learning an important skill that will help them handle emotions, and develop a sense of calmness when they need it most. Learning how to handle pressure can help children, not just in school but everyday settings as well.

The next section will explain how composure can be taught in an online environment. As more and more learning happens in a virtual setting, this skill will become an important one for students to have for successful learning in the future.

HOW CAN KIDS LEARN COMPOSURE IN AN ONLINE SETTING?

When school is conducted in a virtual setting, children are having to learn composure in a whole new way. While a typical classroom has caring teachers, and people who can provide hugs and encouragement, the physical aspect of virtual learning is just different. The following will explain ways that composure can be taught online.

In an online setting, the cameras are typically *on* for both students and teachers. Most do not have the option of turning the camera off as adults sometimes do in meetings. Teachers need to see the learning of students and assess whether they are confused or anxious about the lessons being taught.

They need to read the faces of twenty different squares in a Zoom meeting or a Google Classroom setting. By teaching about composure in an online setting, both kids and educators can benefit.

The first skill that comes to mind when teaching composure in a virtual environment has to do with the technology and adjustments that must be made due to teaching and learning in this setting. Teaching children how to handle a problem with logging in, what to do when the internet suddenly stops working, and how to access the needed tools and platforms that are required in the lessons being taught will be a great first step. Having a plan for handling emergencies and teaching children to take a deep breath will help the students maintain composure and will create far less interruptions in the online learning.

Along with teaching students to take a deep breath to maintain composure while learning online, educators can also teach some simple stress relievers such as counting to ten, having a stress ball or other fidget device, and taking short breaks during the day. Several schools still have a recess time scheduled throughout the school day in which students can log off or simply be away from the computer for a predetermined amount of time. Teachers can encourage students to take a walk, get a snack, and simply have some time to relax during the school day. Just like recess is needed in a typical school setting, students need some unscheduled time as well.

Modeling composure will also help teachers show students how to handle emergencies and glitches when teaching in an online format. When the video does not load, the system suddenly has a lag in the online delivery, or a student needs some attention, modeling the appropriate calmness will help teachers as well. Being able to laugh at oneself and having a backup plan will both help teachers look better prepared as well as calm and composed during the lesson. Students are always looking to the teacher for guidance and calm during pressure and learning/teaching in an online environment is no different. Teachers who do not *lose their cool* when the technology doesn't work will be noticed by the students that they teach.

Parents can also model this same composure while helping their kids learn in an online setting. Having a plan if the home internet goes down, teaching older students to contact their teachers for questions and concerns, and remaining calm and positive during unexpected interruptions will show children how to handle the stress that can accompany online learning. Making the most of planned breaks during the school day and encouraging students to play outside when the weather is permitting will help children receive fresh air and some much needed *down time* during the school day. Allowing students to do these outdoor activities rather than engaging in video games and television will also help the students get away from the overusage of media throughout the day—they are already sitting in front of the screen for the majority of the day, encouraging kids to do something else when the school day is over is an excellent tool for encouraging composure and overall wellness.

All of these skills can help a child not only see the importance of composure in life, but how to attain this skill as well. By working together, teachers and parents can help children learn how to handle emotions and how to develop the skill of composure. Teaching children that it is acceptable to get angry is fine. However, teaching them how to deal with this and remain calm is even better!

KEY IDEAS

- Composure is the ability to stay calm and focused under pressure.
- All people have problems, experience stress, and have accidents. It's how one handles these situations that is important.
- Parents and teachers model composure when bad things occur, and they handle them with calmness and humility, whether in school, at home, or online.
- Looking at characters and real people who are under pressure and discussing how they handle this can also teach the skill of composure.
- Learning stress relief techniques, encouraging outside play, and ways to decrease anxiety are excellent strategies to help children learn composure.
- All adults in a child's life can help teach the skill of composure to children. Learning strategies for handling stress can be used in schools, at home, an in an online setting as well.

Chapter 7

Responsibility

Why is responsibility important to kids?
How can educators teach responsibility to students?
How can parents teach responsibility to children?
How can kids learn responsibility in an online setting?

IMPORTANCE OF RESPONSIBILITY

Responsibility is a soft skill that helps children learn to be accountable, dependable, and conscientious. Responsibility helps children see that their actions and deeds impact others and helps them realize that doing their share of the work makes them accountable to others. Responsibility begins at an early age and can allow children to develop a skill that they will use for the rest of their lives.

Being responsible implies that a student does what he/she is told, follows through with commitments, and does his or her part to contribute to an assignment or project. Teaching kids responsibility means that there are rewards and consequences for getting things done, and that someone will be checking on the progress and completion of certain tasks. Having a parent or teacher check on the progress of chores, assignments, and other commitments means that a child will be held accountable for his or her actions and workload.

Children who learn responsibility at home will be more likely to continue this skill at school and in the future workplace. By learning the skill of follow through and accountability, students will discover that their work is important, and that other people rely on them to complete tasks that are assigned to them. As former advice columnist Abigail Van Buren (Dear Abby) put it, "If you want children to keep their feet on the ground, put some responsibility on their shoulders" (Van Buren n.d.).

By learning to shoulder some responsibility from a young age, children will see the importance of doing their part, learn that they are a part of a

bigger community, and find that following through with chores and assignments is an expectation in order to be successful in the world. Both teachers
and parents can help children learn responsibility and this soft skill should be
a part of every classroom and home.

Teachers who encourage the soft skill of responsibility are those who
assign tasks, expect actions, and hold children accountable for their accomplishments. The following section will examine how teachers can help children learn this skill in the classroom.

HOW CAN EDUCATORS TEACH
RESPONSIBILITY TO CHILDREN?

Teachers are an important factor in teaching responsibility to children. They
can show children the importance of this skill, model it in the classroom
setting, and hold children accountable for their actions. Teaching about the
importance of homework, doing one's part on class projects, and making
students responsible for their own actions is a vital skill that all children
need to learn.

Educators can teach the skill of responsibility by having class chores such
as paper passer, line leader, and class pet feeder. By having roles and responsibilities for the children, teachers can build trust in students, explain the
importance of follow through, and teach students about a sense of community
in the classroom. If all students have a job and must do their part, they will
learn the meaning of working together and the importance of relying on each
other to meet goals and expectations.

Teaching students about the skill of responsibility will allow them to see
the importance of this trait in the real world and will prepare them for future
jobs and obligations. All people in a society have roles they must do, responsibilities that they must undertake, and tasks that are needed to survive. By
teaching children responsibility in the classroom, teachers are preparing their
students to be successful in life. According to the website Proud to be Primary
(2019), "Teaching responsibility in the classroom is important. By teaching
your students to be responsible in the classroom, you're also teaching them to
be responsible at home and in their communities. This is a life skill that they
will need to practice throughout their lives."

Another way that educators can teach responsibility is simply creating an
atmosphere of family and community in the classroom. By creating this type
of environment, teachers model that the classroom is everyone's responsibility. So, at the end of the day, all students clean up the classroom, picking up
trash on the floor—even if it does not belong to them. Having a community
environment also teaches students that they need to work together, help each

other, and be accountable for doing one's best, with the idea that the classroom must work together to succeed.

Emphasizing responsibility in group projects, class commitments, and other undertakings is also a way that teachers can teach this soft skill in the classroom. By doing mini lessons about responsibility, having discussions about what happens when one does not pull one's weight, and talking about how others feel when a student is irresponsible, students can learn first-hand how responsibility impacts both themselves and others.

Dividing the workload accordingly, creating schedules and check-ins, and monitoring the progress of small groups allows the teacher to check on the responsibility of projects and other class endeavors. From kindergarten to high school, children need to see that being a responsible group member is an important skill to have, as children who develop this skill in the early years will become co-workers who follow through with their responsibilities later in life.

A final way that educators can teach responsibility is by expecting that children complete homework, are on time for assignments, and have due dates and expectations for them in the classroom. By establishing such procedures in the classroom, students will know exactly when items are due, will have clear expectations for assignments, and will understand the consequences of being late.

By deducting a few points for late or unfinished assignments, teachers are teaching about the importance of responsibility and follow through in the classroom. Starting in upper elementary grades through high school, students need to learn that being on time is included in the responsibility of homework assignments. Losing a few points for a late penalty teaches children that timeliness is a part of this responsibility as well.

Having policies for turning in late work is an important procedure for the teacher to provide. For example, if a child is ill (or has an excused absence) giving them the number of days absent to complete assignments is a policy that many teachers use. So, if a child is ill for three days, he has three extra days to complete the make-up work without a late penalty. By having procedures in place, teachers have a plan and can communicate these expectations to parents as well.

In the real world, employees are expected to complete jobs and assignments on time. If not, a penalty may be applied, or a person could even lose her job. Adults are expected to pay their bills on time as well. If they don't, a late fee is added to the original bill. By modeling this real-life responsibility of a penalty for being late in the classroom, teachers will be doing their part to prepare students for this soft skill in the future.

For children who are habitually late in assignments, teachers and parents may need to correspond with an extra layer of communication. A parent teacher conference with the child in attendance may be needed to help explain responsibility and create a plan of action. An extra note or assignment notebook may be needed that a teacher signs each afternoon, and a parent reads each evening. For older students, an electronic format such as a gradebook or planner that parents can assess may help them to work on due dates and expectations.

By working together, educators and parents can teach the skill of responsibility to children. Creating both home and school environments where everyone has a role and is accountable is a great way to start. Teaching children about responsibility and helping them learn about commitments to teams, classmates, and others is an important part of this skill. However, teaching this skill at home is just as important. The next section will explain how parents can teach this skill as well.

HOW CAN PARENTS TEACH
RESPONSIBILITY TO CHILDREN?

Parents can begin teaching responsibility to children at a very young age. From the time children are walking and playing, they can be taught to pick up toys and put them back where they belong. Simple skills such as putting things back in their place can be taught as family expectations.

Contributing to the family and having family expectations and chores is also a way for children to learn responsibility in the home. Even the youngest of children can have family chores and show their responsibility and accountability in the household. Young children can set the table, put things away, and help with grocery lists. They can help with the family pets, sweep the sidewalks, and put their clothes away.

Expecting children to help, but not expecting perfection, is the key to teaching young children responsibility. Remembering that they can help with chores and everyday jobs is great. However, remembering that their work may not be perfect is a major key about teaching responsibility at a young age. If a child is supposed to set the table, for example, they may not have the forks in the exact location and the napkins in the correct place in terms of etiquette, but the simple fact that the forks and napkins arrived at the table is the point.

Sometimes adults set the bar a little too high for children. However, noting that we all started somewhere is an important point to remember. If children make an effort, try to do their best, and follow through with what they are told, it is a great start in teaching responsibility. As they continue to do the skill, and gain some maturity, they will get better at the chores assigned to them and will gain self-confidence as a contributing member of the family.

Teaching children about other obligations such as homework and team or club commitments is another part of gaining responsibility. Instructing students about the importance of homework and teaching them a simple routine in the evening will help them learn this skill as a family. Also, learning that being a team player who is accountable and responsible to others is another part of this skill. Showing up for sports practice, completing projects that are assigned, and doing one's part are all components of working with others and learning the importance of responsibility.

Helping others in the family, including younger siblings and even the household pet, are ways that children can contribute to the household and learn responsibility. Having the responsibility of feeding the family dog, helping a little brother, and reading to a younger sister teaches children that they are an important part of the family and have skills that are essential to making everything work.

Doing their part for others and working together as a family are simple ways to teach responsibility at home. Learning that they play an important role in the household, no matter how young they are, can allow children to see how responsibility at home is both significant and valued.

The next section will explore ways to teach responsibility in an online environment. As children are learning more in virtual settings, learning about responsibility in this format will also be a valuable skill. As they enter both college and workplace settings where independent learning and group responsibility are both factors, students need to be prepared for how to use this skill in online learning in addition to classrooms and homes.

HOW CAN KIDS LEARN RESPONSIBILITY IN AN ONLINE SETTING?

Responsibility in an online setting can be a huge key to student success. While a classroom environment provides teachers, who are constantly observing the classroom and monitoring for students who are off task or showing signs of confusion, the online setting creates some challenges in this area. While teachers are doing their best to help students and make sure that they are learning and understanding in virtual classrooms, they are not physically present to look at the work students are completing.

Therefore, teachers need to encourage questions, do multiple checks for understanding, and allow students to share their work and explain their answers. During the pandemic, many teachers set up individual meetings and conferences to make sure that students could have time to ask questions, practice reading aloud to the teacher (for younger students), and check in with the progress of projects and reports for older students. By encouraging students to be responsible for letting a teacher know when they need help, they will learn that this is a major part of responsibility in their own learning.

Students also need to learn to be responsible for completing homework and other projects while learning in an online environment. Again, teachers will not be physically present on a daily basis to check in and look over work. Allowing students to complete projects in stages and providing a checklist of due dates and short-term goals will be very helpful in virtual learning. By providing this calendar, students can check off each part of a longer assignment and work in stages to complete long-term projects. Teachers who create and use such checklists are encouraging responsibility in students, but are also teaching a valuable skill that students can use in both college and the workplace. Since most college classes provide a syllabus and most jobs provide some sort of expected outcomes on long-term projects, this strategy is one that will be used for a lifetime!

Parents can also teach responsibility in an online environment by going over assignments, homework, and due dates with their children at home. Checking the calendar for due dates and marking off completed assignments together will help children become responsible for their own learning and creates a tool that children can use in the future. Younger children will need more parental guidance on this step, but even older students can use a parental check in over dinner.

Parents can also encourage responsibility in an online setting by making sure that children have all of the materials they need, helping them set out items they will need for the next day, and making a list of any materials that are needed for future lessons. By checking for items in advance, rather than the minute they are needed, parents will encourage thinking ahead, which is an important part of being a responsible student.

Finally, parents can model responsibility by sharing ways that they are responsible in their own careers, working collaboratively with teachers, and attending school events such as virtual parent teacher conferences. Showing that they are involved and interested in their child's learning models for them that learning is valued and important, but also displays that they are responsible as well.

Learning in a virtual environment is a strategy that can take responsibility and independence on the part of students, teachers, and parents. It is more than just having the child ready for the school day; it is preparing students to become involved and conscientious as well. By learning the procedures of virtual learning, creating some plans for emergencies like internet disruptions, and using checklists for assignments and due dates, children can become more adept at the soft skill of responsibility even in an online setting.

By working together, both teachers and parents can help children learn responsibility. Through communication about a student's progress, homework concerns, and other child-oriented issues, adults can help children learn that responsibility is important for the future. Working together at school, at home, and online are all ways that kids can learn responsibility that will be needed in college, job settings, and all areas of life. Providing children with ways to learn this important soft skill will encourage planning, preparation, and hopefully success in taking charge and getting things done!

KEY IDEAS

- Responsibility is a skill that children need to learn at an early age as it will be needed for the rest of their lives.
- Responsibility starts in the home by completing simple chores and helping around the house.
- Educators can also teach responsibility by creating a community environment in the classroom (or online) where everyone does his/her part.
- Homework and assignments are a great way to teach responsibility in the classroom.
- Having clear expectations, including penalties for being late, allows teachers to instruct students about responsibility.
- By working together, both parents and teachers can help teach the skill of responsibility to children. This includes responsibility in the home, at school, and in online environments.

Chapter 8

Motivation

Why is motivation important to kids?
How can educators teach motivation to students?
How can parents teach motivation to children?
How can kids learn motivation in an online setting?

IMPORTANCE OF MOTIVATION

Motivation is another soft skill that is important for children to learn. According to Gopalan et al. (2017), "The working definition of motivation is a persuasive feeling that always provides positivism to students to accomplish a task or activity to the end and succeed in it no matter how hard and tough it is."

Motivation applies to all areas of a child's life and includes motivation to accomplish a task at home, motivation to complete a project at school, and motivation to follow one's dreams—both in one's personal life and one's career. Teaching children the skill of motivation can be tricky as there is no set prescription or guide for how to do this.

Children often learn motivation by seeing someone who is inspirational, encouraging, and influential. It could be a parent or relative, a famous person, or a teacher. Regardless of the person who provides this motivation to children, learning to be positive, complete the tasks assigned, and be successful are key. Even during hard times and roadblocks, students who learn the skill of motivation are those that persevere and reach goals, regardless of the barriers they face.

Motivation is often thought of as a skill that is practiced in schools and workplaces, as people complete courses, succeed in jobs, and complete goals. However, it also applies to one's home and personal life as well. Even young children can learn the skill of motivation as they persevere when building a tower of blocks, learn to read, and accomplish the skill of tying their shoes.

Starting with these small tasks, both parents and teachers can encourage their determination, perseverance, and eventual success.

By encouraging, praising, and noticing even the small steps in a child's accomplishments and setting goals which are both realistic and developmentally appropriate, both parents and teachers can help their children foster the soft skill of motivation. By encouraging small successes, learning to take baby steps, and working toward an attainable goal, adults can help children see that working hard and doing one's best will eventually pay off.

While the goal of motivation is to teach the child to learn self-motivation, learning this skill through the guidance of adults is the best way to start. Children do not arrive in the world being intrinsically motivated and knowing the steps needed to accomplish their goals. However, with the guidance of parents and teachers, they can learn how to persevere, work hard, and make goals happen.

Intrinsic motivation, or the idea that one achieves simply because one has the desire and will to do so without the need for rewards and praise, is the ultimate goal of motivation in children. While young children may need praise or a sticker for accomplishing a goal or returning their homework, they ultimately need to learn the skill of being intrinsically motivated to do their personal best in anything they choose to do.

While motivation may seem like a simple skill that all children need, teaching them to attain the intrinsic motivation that is necessary to succeed in adulthood is something that takes both time and effort from teachers and parents. The following section will tell how teachers can explain and model this skill in the classroom.

HOW CAN EDUCATORS TEACH MOTIVATION TO CHILDREN?

Teachers are an influential part of learning motivation. Teachers who set high expectations, develop relationships with their students, and learn about their strengths and interests can encourage their students in areas that excite and interest them. By motivating children to do their best, take risks in their learning, and set realistic goals, teachers can model that hard work and perseverance are an important skill for children.

Creating classroom environments in which children are allowed ownership of their learning, encouraged to try new things, and allowed to make mistakes enables teachers to promote motivation in their students' learning. Because motivation is one of the most important parts of engaging students in the classroom, this skill is important for all teachers to develop. The website Teach.com (2019) states that:

One of the most difficult aspects of becoming a teacher is learning how to motivate your students. It is also one of the most important. Students who are not motivated will not learn effectively. They won't retain information, they won't participate and some of them may even become disruptive.

By creating an environment of acceptance, encouraging students to do their best, and allowing students to pursue their interests and ambitions, teachers will motivate children to persevere and do their best in their learning.

Teachers can also motivate children to become involved in their learning by making lessons fun, interesting, and exciting to children. By doing hands-on activities instead of worksheets, allowing children to make choices in how they demonstrate their learning, and creating a fun atmosphere, teachers will model that learning is enjoyable and interesting. Effort put forth by a teacher to accomplish these goals is never wasted as children learn best when they are active and involved.

Encouragement and praise are also important factors in developing motivation in children. When teachers encourage students to do their best and are optimistic about doing well in their assignments, they are apt to do the same thing in their future. Teachers who are kind, reassuring, and positive will create students who are willing to take risks and are not afraid to make mistakes.

Helping children to set realistic goals, differentiating instruction to help children be successful, and creating materials that are interesting and motivating will help students realize their potential, and learn the skill of motivation. Doing boring, dull, uninteresting activities will not promote enthusiasm for learning, and can actually hinder the development of motivation in children. Teachers who create fun learning opportunities are more likely to develop learners who are motivated and excited to learn.

Teachers also need to learn when to ask for help from others when a student is deemed as unmotivated. Talking to parents to find out about challenges the child might be facing, allowing parents to suggest ideas that might help or encourage learning, and working with others such as the school counselor can help teachers determine why motivation might be lacking and to find ways to encourage even the most unmotivated learner.

Knowing when to reach out for assistance, discovering ways that students learn best, and involving parents and families in the learning can help teachers motivate learners and encourage families to contribute as well. Since parents are the child's first teacher, allowing parents to participate in their learning, offer suggestions that are motivating, and suggest ways that might help a teacher are all wonderful ideas for reaching unmotivated learners.

In conclusion, motivation is a skill that takes perseverance, dedication, and optimism to learn. Teachers who are encouraging, interesting, and allow students to take risks and make mistakes are those who children will remember as their coaches, cheerleaders, and influencers. By allowing students to explore their areas of interests, accommodating for various learning styles, and creating lessons that are interactive and fun, teachers can help students learn self-motivation and a love for learning that will last a lifetime.

Parents are vital to teaching about motivation as well. By working together with teachers, they can help children learn about motivation. The following ideas can be used by parents to teach this soft skill in the home.

HOW CAN PARENTS TEACH MOTIVATION TO CHILDREN?

Teaching children to be motivated is a skill that parents can begin at a very young age. When parents encourage a child to take her first steps, pick up the toys after playing with them, and get dressed with no assistance, they are teaching their children to work hard and accomplish their goals. Even though these items may seem trivial, children learn at a young age that if they do things on their own, people notice.

Noticing and praising children for their accomplishments is one of the most important things parents can do to teach children the soft skill of motivation. When we have parents coaching us to succeed, we want to do more to show them our accomplishments. Children of all ages work harder when they are encouraged, motivated, and stimulated to do well.

While young children may need stickers for doing daily chores, or accomplishing small tasks around the home, older students eventually need to be intrinsically motivated. In other words, children need to eventually learn to do tasks simply because they are expectations for the family to be successful. Feeding the dog, not because one gets a sticker, but because it is one's family responsibility is an example of intrinsic motivation.

Doing chores because they are the right thing to do or working for good grades in school because one wants to be successful in life are both examples of intrinsic motivation. They are both important tasks and both display a sense of maturity in children when they learn to work toward goals for personal fulfillment or responsibility and not simply for rewards and praise.

Learning personal satisfaction can go a long way in developing the skill of motivation in children. Renee Bacher, author of the article "6 ways to Motivate your Children" (2019), states, "Encourage him to follow the lead of what makes him feel good inside—such as satisfaction in a newly learned skill or a job well done. He's not only more successful in the long term, he's also happy along the way, and inspired."

By teaching children to learn how to accomplish goals, gaining satisfaction for a job well done, and being inspired simply by doing one's best, children will learn the beginning skills of motivation. These preliminary skills, and the feeling of being successful create a beginning for the soft skill of motivation.

As children get older, learning to be motivated by their interests and strengths is another way that parents can encourage motivation in children. Children who love a specific hobby or want to play a musical instrument will learn motivation as they engage in a new skill, practice what they learned, and are successful in doing what they love to do.

Motivation in school is also an important factor for parents to encourage and stimulate. Parents who show an interest in school, help with homework, and are active in a child's education are modeling the importance of school-work in a child's life. Reading to a child, discussing what the child is learning, and taking an active interest in school are simple and inexpensive ways that a parent can promote and encourage education at home.

Noticing when a child receives a good grade on a test, brings home a great report card, or even shows improvement in a subject that a child struggles with are all ways that a parent can promote motivation and the importance of education in a child's life. When children receive praise and encouragement from their parents, they are more likely to do better in school and have a positive attitude toward learning.

Parents can model motivation as well. When parents show their motivation in jobs, personal goals, and accomplishments, children will see this skill in action and are likely to follow this model as well. By sharing accomplishments from work, goals about personal interests, and ideas about how to reach these goals, children will see the value of working hard and being motivated to do well. Overall, parents who encourage children to take risks, do their best, and achieve goals that are realistic in nature will motivate children to do well and reach their aspirations in life.

The next section will explain ways to encourage and teach the soft skill of motivation in an online environment as well. Being motivated to learn in an online setting is important as students are learning more frequently in this format.

HOW CAN KIDS LEARN MOTIVATION ONLINE?

During the pandemic of 2019–2021, many schools were forced to move to an online format and many students were required to show up for learning in their new environment. Of all of the soft skills mentioned in this book, this is the one that probably concerned people the most! Young children were often anxious about learning in a new format that was removed from friends and lacked the human touch. Older students often lacked motivation when they had to move to more of an independent strategy of learning. Teachers and parents alike reported students not showing up for synchronous class learning and not completing required assignments and projects. The simple fact that students were learning from home and often alone created many issues for students in this situation.

Teachers can help with the motivation part of online learning by providing hands-on lessons, making teaching interesting, and taking the time to build relationships with the students in one's class. The more interesting and interactive a teacher can make lessons the more likely students are to show up for class! Students who are bored, uninterested, and indifferent to learning will not be motivated to learn either. By taking the time to connect with students, build relationships, and get to know the students in their class, teachers are more likely to have students attend class and want to learn.

Also, student involvement, even in an online environment, is crucial to helping students be motivated to learn. If a teacher can create interactive lessons that involve students and allow them to participate, the children will be far more motivated than simply showing up to attend a lecture!

Teachers can also encourage motivation by creating challenges, competitions, and games that allow students to be involved and participative in the learning. During recent online classes at the college level, I created writing competitions each week during the pandemic and mailed restaurant gift cards to my students each week. Realizing that motivation was especially tough while teaching during a pandemic, this small action helped encourage students to show up and participate in lessons each week.

Parents can help encourage motivation at home as well. Even though kids are not leaving their houses for school each day, parents can motivate students to learn by providing rewards and competitions at home. Creating a friendly competition at home among siblings for who completed their homework first, who logged on to class first, and who read the most pages that week can be helpful as well. Even prizes such as choosing the next family movie or Friday's dinner menu can be helpful in motivating students to learn.

Motivation at home can also be encouraged by discussing topics from classes in the evenings—after school hours. Since the interaction with teachers is most likely more limited when students are solely learning online, taking a few minutes at dinner time or while riding in the car to share what the kids are working on, what they are learning, and their favorite part of the school day can make up for this. Parents and preschool-age children can certainly share the highlights of their work or home days as well.

The key here is to genuinely listen, ask questions that enhance the conversation, and in turn motivate children to attend class the following day. By sharing what they learned, kids are able to communicate this new information, see a purpose for the learning, and be more motivated to learn. Also, helping students make meaningful connections to real-life situations can create a motivation to learn as well. If they understand how the skills they are learning are used in the real world they will see the worth and value of their assignments and homework each day.

By creating interesting online lessons, building positive relationships, and pointing out the importance of lessons in real-world settings, both teachers and parents can encourage and participate in the learning of children. They can also motivate them to learn by checking in on their progress, listening to new information over dinner, and creating friendly competitions both at school and at home. By helping students see the importance and value of learning and looking for the fun in everything, students will be more motivated to learn and succeed in their online learning efforts.

KEY IDEAS

- Motivation is the idea of working hard and persevering even if the task is difficult.
- Encouragement and praise are both ways to develop motivation in children, whether in classrooms or online.
- Parents can teach motivation by inspiring children to do their best and noticing even small accomplishments.
- Teaching the concept of intrinsic motivation is an important goal for children to learn.
- Teachers can model and encourage motivation in their classrooms as well by creating interesting lessons and creating friendly competitions both in person and online.
- Parents and teachers can work together to encourage children to succeed and do well in their endeavors.

Chapter 9

Resilience

Why is the skill of resilience important to kids?
How can educators teach the skill of resilience to students?
How can parents teach the skill of resilience to children?
How can resilience be taught in an online setting?

IMPORTANCE OF RESILIENCE

Resilience is a soft skill that children need to succeed in today's world. According to Dictionary.com (2019) resilience is the "ability to recover readily from illness, depression, adversity, or the like." Resilience is being able to *bounce back* after bad things happen. It is remaining positive even through the rough times and having the *grit* to keep trying even after failure. Resilience means that kids may have an interruption or difficulty in their lives but can learn to continue with their lifestyle despite any adversity they encountered.

Kids today have a lot to deal with. They must do well in school, take care of family commitments, and participate in extracurricular activities. There is a great deal of pressure to succeed, whether that be by maintaining a certain grade point average, kicking the game-winning field goal, or earning badges in scouting activities. Many children put pressure on themselves to succeed and parents and teachers often add to this load as well.

But what happens when a major life event happens such as the death of a parent, a divorce in the family, or a mother who is deployed in the military? Children need to have the guidance and strength to still be successful, overcome obstacles, and have the support necessary to keep going with their daily lives.

Knowing the abilities and characteristics of children and being able to support them through the tough times is where resilience comes in. In stressful times, children will react differently. Some will become very quiet, some will need constant reassurance, and still others will just shut down. Being kind, nurturing, and compassionate to the child's needs is a key factor in helping them. If a child needs to cry, yell, or scream—let him. If a child needs to draw a quiet picture, self-soothe, and remain quiet—allow her to do so. In other words, allow children to grieve in their own way, while providing support and a loving home or school environment in which to do so.

While major life changes such as death, divorce, or illness are often a precursor to resilience, sometimes, something as simple as a problem with friendships, a family move, or difficulty with schoolwork or a sports team can cause a child to need the skill of resilience. Even though these events may seem ordinary to adults, they can cause confusion, anxiety, and sleepless nights for children. Being aware of these problems as an adult can help one to provide guidance and reassurance to a child who is struggling.

By teaching the skill of resilience to children, teachers and parents can help them learn coping skills, stress relief strategies, and survival skills—even when the world seems to be crumbling around them. Teachers and parents who model this skill themselves and have an optimistic outlook are the first part of teaching resilience to children. The next section will explain how educators can teach this skill in the classroom.

HOW CAN EDUCATORS TEACH RESILIENCE TO CHILDREN?

Teachers can teach and model the skill of resilience in the classroom setting. By being aware of the normal behaviors and actions of students, a good teacher will be able to notice when a child is not behaving normally or seems upset about something. A quick conversation and a listening ear can help the teacher determine if a child needs help, if a parent contact might be needed, or if there is something in the classroom that is causing a child to be anxious or upset.

Having a good relationship with the school counselor or other experts at the school will enable a teacher to work collectively with others if a child experiences a traumatic experience such as the illness of a parent. Also, encouraging parents to keep the teacher informed of changes in the schedule and lifestyle of children is a great way to keep the lines of communication open between school and home.

Teaching social skills such as problem solving, anti-bullying strategies, and conflict resolution are also strategies that can be taught and implemented in the classroom. By giving students the *power of words*, teachers emphasize that communicating about problems and standing up for oneself and others in today's world. Also, teaching students what to do if they have issues or problems with others is an important part of this strategy.

Surrounding the students with positive posters and quotes such as Epictetus' "It's not what happens to you, but how you react to it that matters" (no date) is another way that teachers can reinforce the skill of resilience in the classroom. Creating an atmosphere of kindness, acceptance, and community will enable children to feel comfortable talking to others about problems they may be having and can create a support system as well. Sometimes just knowing that one is not alone can help children be more resilient in the face of adversity.

Doing stress relief activities such as yoga for children, brain breaks, and other quick activities are ways that teachers can promote healthy lifestyles, and teach children coping skills when they encounter stressful situations. While these strategies will not cure every stressful time in a child's life, having these tools will possibly enable the minor problems to be de-escalated before they become larger.

Allowing children to simply have free time and a break when needed can also help children learn the skill of resiliency. When a child is dealing with a problem at home or school simply allowing a *time out* that is not accompanied by a consequence or penalty is a welcome idea for such students. Sometimes an extra bathroom break, a walk in the hallway, or a quiet place in the classroom can do wonders for getting a child back on track in the daily routine of the classroom. As long as children are not taking advantage of such situations, allowing these breaks can help them get away from the stressors—if even for a few minutes.

Reading about famous people who faced adversity and overcame obstacles is another way that children can learn about the skill of resiliency. Discussing the tools and approaches that the people used to overcome their problems is a way to model these same approaches to children. Discussing and developing skills such as perseverance and determination are skills that can help children survive—both in third grade and in life!

Teachers who are aware of the normal behaviors of their students, know when to intervene, and create partnerships with parents and other school employees can help children who are experiencing anxiety and stress in their lives. By being approachable, kind, and welcoming, children are more apt to tell teachers when something is bothering them.

Relaxation skills, stress relief strategies and problem-solving methods are also useful tools for teaching resilience. Finally, creating an environment of acceptance and learning about others who overcame obstacles can be useful in the classroom as well.

By communicating with parents and families, being willing to work with others, and offering support and encouragement when children are going through trying times, teachers can help teach the skill of resiliency in students. The world has many problems and stressors, even for the youngest children. Learning how to cope and work through them is a soft skill that children need in today's world. The next section will provide examples of how parents can help as well.

HOW CAN PARENTS TEACH RESILIENCE TO CHILDREN?

Parents are often the first to notice stress and anxiety in children. They may not have the appetite that they used to, may have trouble sleeping, or show signs of sadness or depression. In the event of a major life change such as the death of a grandparent, an illness in the family, or an upcoming separation from a family member, parents are likely to know the cause of this stress and be able to provide reassurance, extra hugs, and nurturing to their kids.

However, not all stressors in life are as apparent to parents and caregivers. Sometimes, difficulty in school, a problem with peers, and anxiety about activities can also cause stress in children. There may not be one obvious trigger but being in tune with a child's normal activities and behaviors can help a parent realize that something is wrong in a child's life. In the *Handbook of Resilience in Children* (2014), Goldstein and Brooks state:

> The perception that no child is immune from pressure in our current, fast-paced, stress filled environment, an environment we have created to prepare children to become functional adults. Even children fortunate to not face significant adversity or trauma or be burdened by intense stress or anxiety, experience the pressures around them and the expectations placed upon them.

Being open, approachable, and honest with children can help them identify the stressors and reasons that they may be feeling nervous or anxious. Helping them brainstorm a list of solutions, and taking ownership of the problem, can help them to learn coping skills, develop strategies, and implement new plans to help them be successful and alleviate the problems in their lives.

When children have adversity in their lives, even the smallest problem can develop into a big one. Helping children overcome this adversity, regardless what the source of the problem is, is helping children to be resilient. Parents who take the time to listen and are willing to help children with their problems are those who can help them learn to cope with stress and overcome their problems.

At the same time, parents need to know when a simple talk or brainstorming session to come up with some problem-solving ideas are just not enough. A child who is having difficulty managing every day activities, and is stressed beyond what is normal for them, may need professional help through a counselor, psychologist, or therapist who specializes in the needs of children. Starting with the family doctor is a great way to get recommendations and find resources for making this happen.

Acknowledging when a problem is beyond the extra support and reassurance of a parent or family member is not a sign of weakness. It simply means that another person may be more effective in helping the child to be resilient and learn to cope with their adversity. Asking for help from an additional person such as a counselor or therapist is also a great way for parents to model that one does not have to tackle their problems alone. Building a support system for the child and encouraging him/her to seek solutions with the help of others is an admirable trait in parents.

Communicating concerns and issues to teachers, involving a school counselor, and requesting support from the school and community are also ways that parents can get the help they need when their child is exhibiting signs of trauma or anxiety. Keeping teachers informed when a parent or grandparent is ill, sharing the news of an expected new sibling, or simply letting others know about changes in a child's life will alert adults to keep an extra eye on the student and be prepared for any sudden disruptions in the behavior and normal routines of children.

By working together as a team, parents and teachers can help a child by being on the same page, communicating the same plans for assistance, and exercising consistent expectations. Guiding children through both everyday issues and major problems in life will help them learn to persevere and learn the skill of resilience.

Students can also learn the skill of resilience in an online setting. When the pandemic hit during the spring of 2020, many students were suddenly faced with learning online as their schools closed and their learning shifted online. Students became resilient in ways that teachers and parents never thought of. The next section will explain how to teach this soft skill in an online environment.

HOW CAN KIDS LEARN RESILIENCE ONLINE?

Resilience is the soft skill which defines children who bounce back from adversity and learn to be successful after an event or problem in their lives. Dealing with adversity and learning to look for the positive parts of life indeed happens in online learning as well. When many schools closed during the spring of 2020 for the COVID-19 pandemic, children quickly learned a new format for school, became separated from friends, and had to adapt to learning at home, with parents as teachers. The fact that children survived, returned to school, and continued on their academic journey is proof in itself that students are resilient!

Teachers can work on the idea of resilience in the online environment by continually pointing out the progress students have made (as opposed to pointing out that they might be behind in their academics compared to previous school years). According to Shapiro (2021) in an article about post-pandemic teaching she states:

> There is no finish line for learning; it's a process. We must expect that children won't necessarily be at the same level of learning that they were last year or even the year before. While this will likely frustrate everyone involved at points along the learning process, I advise that this should be considered when creating the new classroom curriculum to ensure that students are getting a refresh on complex topics to reduce any discouragement.

By encouraging students to do their best, not comparing curriculum timelines to previous years, and helping children to be successful in an online environment, teachers can do a great deal to promote resiliency in our students. Simply sharing that students *are* learning and growing in their schooling, regardless of format, can go far in encouraging students to do their best.

Teachers can also promote resilience in students by sharing progress and success in meaningful ways. Sending emails to families, discussing the class's progress on assignments and assessments, and praising students for the work and effort they are doing can also go far in helping kids see that they are indeed learning and growing and resilient in their own small ways.

Finally, teachers can teach the skill of resilience by teaching coping skills and stress relievers during the school day, even if the school day is online. Remembering to take brain breaks, allowing the students a few minutes to stretch, or even having an online *dance party* can do wonders for helping students remain on task and resilient in an online environment.

Parents can help with the skill of resilience by helping kids see the progress they have made and the goals that they have reached in a virtual environment. Helping children see their growth and learning in both school and personal goals can show them how to be successful, even if their schools were not in a typical setting or format. They can also communicate with teachers if a child is showing signs of stress or anxiety that come from learning in a different format. If a child is not doing as well learning online or is having difficulty paying attention or focusing, they should contact the teacher to develop a plan for some extra breaks or other coping strategies to help the students be successful in their learning.

Parents can also help students learn the skill of resilience by pointing out people that they know, or people in the news, who are survivors and have perseverance. People who were diagnosed with COVID, yet survived, front line workers who went to work every day during a pandemic, and even athletes who were in the Olympics and faced adversity can be shared with students. Seeing real-life examples of grit and determination can help students see that hard work and a positive attitude can help them overcome obstacles and continue on their path toward learning.

By learning the skill of resilience at an early age, children will be better prepared for both college and career-related experiences that they will encounter in the future. They will learn that they can fall down but get back up, that they can fail and then succeed, and that mistakes are part of the learning process. Learning resilience both at home and at school will help children be better prepared to meet the needs of the future and to face them in realistic ways, with an optimistic attitude. All students face adversity and all children encounter problems and challenges in life. However, it is what they do in these circumstances that makes a difference. Learning to be resilient has both a purpose and a meaning to those who are survivors and overcome the bad things in life. Teaching this soft skill to students will prepare them for many obstacles in their lives and education.

KEY IDEAS

- Resilience is the idea that children can recover from problems and adversity.
- Adversity can come in the form of major life changes such as illness, death of a family member, and divorce. However, it can also be in the form of smaller stressors like schoolwork and friendship issues.
- Teachers can help teach resilience by modeling and teaching coping strategies in the classroom and in an online environment.
- Parents need to be aware of changes in their child and be willing to accept help if needed.
- Parents and teachers need to communicate and create a team plan for helping children who are experiencing stress and anxiety, whether this is in a typical classroom setting or a virtual one.
- Resilience is a soft skill that children will use forever and a skill that will help them be successful in all areas of their lives.

Chapter 10

Integrity

Why is integrity an important skill for kids?
How can educators teach the skill of integrity to students?
How can parents teach the skill of integrity to children?
How do kids learn integrity in an online setting?

IMPORTANCE OF INTEGRITY

The famous author C.S. Lewis once said, "Integrity is doing the right thing even when no one is watching" (Lewis n.d.). Integrity includes items such as honesty, values, and compassion. It means teaching a child to be ethical, make good choices, and practice sincerity. Integrity also involves putting yourself in someone else's shoes and thinking about how you would feel in a similar situation. The skill of integrity is one that children learn by being around good people who model good choices in their everyday lives.

Integrity is modeling one's beliefs and values and making decisions that accompany these values. It is not just talking about being a good and honest person, it is about making the choices that *show* one is a good and honest person. It is about establishing a system of beliefs and ethics and living them in one's daily life.

Children learn integrity through the examples of their caregivers and by being placed in difficult situations in which they must make decisions that will impact others. Learning the ideas of empathy and compassion can accompany the skill of integrity, as one's choices impact everyone around them. Knowing that *actions speak louder than words* and do not just impact one person are lessons that children need to learn at an early age.

Integrity also includes being a good person, even in the absence of parents and teachers. It is making the right choices with a group of friends, finding money on the floor and turning it in, or helping someone without being told.

Integrity is when children do the right thing, without thinking about rewards and praise, but simply because it is the moral thing to do.

Teachers, parents, and any adult in a child's life can model and teach the skill of integrity. Although some families may choose to develop this skill in a faith-based setting such as a church or synagogue, integrity can also be learned in everyday life. When a child makes a poor decision or makes an ill-advised choice, adults can help guide the child to a better option and can emphasize the importance of this choice as it impacts the child and others.

Teaching integrity is done by adults who model the skill themselves, by being kind and moral people. They show children integrity simply by being good people and making proper choices in their daily lives. They also help children learn from difficult situations and guide them to make better choices after a misbehavior.

By helping children learn the soft skill of integrity, teachers and parents will raise children who make good choices, do the right thing, and are ethical citizens. Learning integrity helps children learn about the norms and rules of society while developing good and just human beings as well. The following section will explain ways that integrity can be taught in the classroom.

HOW CAN EDUCATORS TEACH INTEGRITY TO CHILDREN?

Teachers can show and model the soft skill of integrity in their classrooms. By displaying kindness and compassion to others, modeling correct behaviors for children, and guiding students in their decision making and choices, they can show them the proper actions and alternatives for a school setting. Setting a good example for the children in one's classroom models both respect and integrity in the teaching profession.

Teachers are an important part of this soft skill because they are constantly modeling and being viewed by the children in the classroom. If they see their teacher doing the right thing, they are more apt to make this choice as well. For example, teachers who choose to follow the school rules such as not chewing gum in the classroom are showing children that they respect and abide by these rules, and not that they apply only to kids.

Modeling the skill of integrity is also done on a daily basis in the way that teachers treat and value the children in their classrooms. Treating each child with kindness, respecting all students, and avoiding favoritism are all actions that students notice. Doing one's best to be reasonable and unbiased, (and being able to explain one's actions in special circumstances) is important for teachers to do in their classrooms.

Along with these actions are the ideas of fairness and consistency in the classroom. In an article in *Psychology Today* (2015), Price-Mitchell states that "While teachers cannot control student behavior, they can respond with *consistency* when enforcing school and classroom policies. In a classroom culture that places learning first, dishonest behavior is a teachable moment."

Dealing with inappropriate behaviors in the classroom is a way that a teacher can use teachable moments and help children to learn better choices the next time a person is in the same predicament. Mistakes and poor choices happen in classrooms, from pre-K through college, however, how a teacher handles these circumstances is key. Helping children learn why an action was wrong, how it impacted others, and how to make a better decision in the future are all ways that a teacher can assist in the teaching of integrity.

Teaching social skills such as decision making, honesty, and compassion are also strategies that teachers can use in the classroom. Noticing when a child makes a good decision or does the right thing is a wonderful way to begin this process in the classroom. When a teacher notices proper behavior in the classroom, it tends to have a *ripple effect* and will be noticed and copied by others in the classroom.

Reading about literary characters or talking about real people who have shown acts of integrity are also strategies for teaching this skill in the classroom. Many characters in books, both real and fictional, face choices in their lives. Reading and discussing these choices with children are tools for creating an understanding of integrity in the classroom. Asking why the character chose to *do the right thing* can create a lesson about why integrity matters both in the classroom and in life.

Telling children about a story in the news such as a person who finds a large sum of money and returns it to the owner is another way to teach integrity to children. Discussing why returning the money instead of keeping it (even though it was really tempting) is a great way to explain the importance of right from wrong and how one's actions impact others.

Playing games and doing activities such as *What Would You Do?*, where a teacher explains a situation and asks the students what they would do in certain situations, are more ways to teach and model integrity in the classroom. Scenarios such as *you catch a friend cheating on a test* can be discussed by the teacher and students can share answers and explanations about what they would do and why. Asking guiding questions and allowing the students to discuss in a non-judgmental environment can help guide children in this process.

Overall, the soft skill of integrity is one that is needed in all aspects of life. Being a kind and moral person, making good decisions and ethical choices, and being fair to others are all characteristics that will help children be successful in life. By learning about integrity in academic settings, children will be able to carry this skill with them into their future. However, by involving parents, this skill can be emphasized even more. The next section will explain ways that parents can teach integrity in the home.

HOW CAN PARENTS TEACH INTEGRITY TO CHILDREN?

Parents begin teaching integrity from the time children are little, simply by being good people themselves. Such parents model proper ethical behaviors, make good choices, and consider the feelings of others when they make decisions. They do the right things, without considering rewards or recognition, and consider how their actions impact the lives of others.

Parents can create homes with integrity by having a set of rules and guidelines for their children. Such homes have curfews and check-ins, monitor television and video games, and allow children privileges that are based on age and maturity. As children show maturity and good choices in their lives, they earn more opportunities and privileges.

By not simply allowing children to do what they want, and gradually releasing privileges as they earn them, parents are modeling that children who make proper choices are allowed to do more mature and exciting things. This part of integrity is one that varies in households but is a great way for children to learn that by making the right choices, they can earn even greater privileges.

Parents can teach integrity by having difficult conversations with their children. When friends are allowed to stay up without bedtimes, play inappropriate video games, and do behaviors that are not acceptable in other families, children will often use the phrase, *"But so and so is allowed to do it!"*

By having conversations about why some behaviors are not allowed in their homes, and why some activities are not acceptable to their parents, children will begin developing the moral background that they need to have in place to become compassionate adults who make good decisions. Sometimes explaining that all families do not make the same choices for their children is a good way to explain differences in parenting and belief systems. Remembering to not place blame on parents who make other decisions, but simply saying that their parents love their children and want them to be good people, is a nice way to explain this to children—though it's a conversation that may need to be repeated several times!

Having conversations about people in the news or situations in which children make inappropriate choices is another way to teach integrity to children. Talking about what the people did wrong and how they could have made better choices the next time exhibits a way to teach good decision-making skills in children. Emphasizing the idea of *learning from one's mistakes* can be a valuable tool for parents to use in such conversations.

As children get older, they will even bring situations of poor choices to the dinner table. School-age children like to report about the bad choices of others to their parents, tell about things that were done, and kids who got *in trouble.* Being able to debrief about such incidents and talk about ways the children could have made better choices can explain and teach the skill of integrity by using real-world examples.

Teenagers often point out students who are in trouble at school as well. Telling parents about situations from other students who are expelled and in trouble with the law is often a sign that they need approval and acknowledgment for not being in the same situation. Appreciating and valuing the proper choices of one's own children is another way that parents can confirm that their children are making the correct choices and actions.

Sometimes, just being available to listen to the children in our lives is a way that adults can help children learn the skill of integrity. Having a willing listener, who will help guide children to proper decisions and choices, is one of the best ways that children can learn right from wrong. They often know the right choices, but simply need the validation and respect from adults to do so. Integrity is also a skill that can be learned in an online setting. Students who are learning from home or an alternate location while doing online assignments can develop this skill in several ways. The next section will define several strategies to learn integrity in an online setting.

HOW CAN KIDS LEARN INTEGRITY IN AN ONLINE SETTING?

Learning in a virtual environment presents problems and concerns that are not present in a typical classroom. One of the most interesting of these problems is the idea of academic integrity—if a child is working online can he/she just look up the information and *cheat?* Having a huge amount of information and resources available online or on a cell phone and not having a teacher who is constantly monitoring the learning of students can both create concerns for online learning. In a typical classroom environment, a teacher is constantly roving and monitoring student work and making sure that they are not using outside resources in their answers.

However, in an online environment, this can be a bit more difficult. Teachers who are instructing virtually need to establish guidelines for what is acceptable and not acceptable in assignments and projects. Are students allowed to Google answers, look up information on cell phones, or even ask parents for answers during their virtual learning? Some teachers will not mind if students do this, as it allows students to use their available resources in their learning. However, others will not encourage this at all. Being sure to set parameters for when the students should be working on their own and when they are allowed to use outside resources will be important to both the teacher and the students.

Another way that teachers can teach the skill of integrity in an online setting is by explaining expectations for learning and confidentiality in a virtual classroom. While teachers typically do not share which students are struggling and which are excelling, this may become more apparent when all students are visible in a Zoom meeting or Google classroom. Having a discussion about how students learn differently and that we all have both strengths and struggles can help teachers explain this concept to students. While trying to maintain confidentiality is important in an online environment, it is simply a bit more open for others to see progress and understanding when the children all show up on a computer screen! Discussing this important concept is also important to cover at the beginning of the school year.

Parents can also help with the skill of integrity in an online class. Checking on the parameters of assignments, reading the directions carefully with children, and noting whether outside help is allowed or not can help students navigate their learning in a format that may not be familiar to them. Also, frequent checks on students during the day can help parents monitor the online learning as well. From kindergarten students who may simply need help with logging onto the computer to high school students who may need assistance in defining plagiarism and how much help they can have on assignments, knowing that parents are offering guidance and advice can be both welcoming and reassuring to students.

Parents can also model integrity online by sharing about situations that they encounter while working online for their personal jobs. Explaining the importance of doing one's own work, cooperating with others in a professional way, and modeling integrity in the virtual workplace can help students see the importance of this soft skill as well.

Integrity is a skill that children learn by watching those around them. They gain this skill by watching their parents and families and by observing the values and ethics in their homes and those of their peers. Children learn integrity by talking about their decisions and those of people they see in the news. They also learn integrity by making choices—some good and some bad. Kids learn integrity by choosing to do their own work in a virtual environment rather than Googling all of the answers. Learning how to use this skill will enable kids to make good decisions that are based on doing the right things in life.

KEY IDEAS

- Integrity means making the right choices, even when no one is watching.
- Integrity is teaching children to do the right thing in difficult situations.
- Teachers can model integrity by displaying consistency and fairness in their classrooms and in online settings.
- Teachers can also instruct about integrity by using teachable moments, real-life situations, and characters in books who make good decisions.
- Parents can teach integrity by modeling ethical behaviors and talking about the choices that people make in their lives.
- By working together, both parents and educators can help teach this skill to children, regardless of the format in which they are learning.

Chapter 11

Organization

Why is the skill of organization important to kids?
How can educators teach this skill to students?
How can parents teach organization skills to children?
How can kids learn organization in an online setting?

IMPORTANCE OF ORGANIZATION

Organization is a skill that all people, regardless of age, need to have. Organization helps one feel safe, prepared, and ready for the day ahead. It implies that you care about your studies or your job, and it helps you stand out in the classroom and career world. Organization is often not noticed—until it is lacking.

Students who are lacking in organization skills are those who can't find assignments, have messy desks, and often forget due dates and appointments. They sometimes misplace their backpacks, owe overdue fees at the library for lost books, and often look disheveled. According to Morin of Understood.Org (2019), an advocacy group for children with attention and learning needs:

> Kids who have weak organization skills struggle with handling information in an effective and logical way. They often have difficulty setting priorities, making plans, sticking to a task and getting things done. These skills become increasingly important as your child moves through different grade levels.

Organization is a skill that can be taught and nurtured in the K-12 classroom and is important for parents and teachers to work on together. By teaching children organization, they will be more successful in school, will stick to projects and tasks, and will likely get better grades. It is hard to turn in assignments that are lost and forgotten.

While parents and teachers are often frustrated with children who lack organization skills, there is hope for teaching this skill to children. Organization takes some time and a few supplies such as calendars, labels, and notebooks to achieve. However, the time and money invested in teaching children to be organized is well worth the effort.

Sometimes parents and teachers say that "organization is just not their thing" or "I'm not organized but I get to work everyday." While this may be true, the more organized their children become, the more successful they will be in school. Preparing students for the skills and expectations of the school day and making sure children are ready with materials and assignments can make the school day go smoother for the students and is far less stressful than spending the day looking for things.

Teaching organization skills may seem like a minor problem for some children; however, this skill is vital to a student's success—both in the classroom and in their future for college and careers. Children who learn organization skills at an early age will be more successful in learning and in life.

HOW CAN EDUCATORS TEACH
THIS SKILL TO CHILDREN?

Teachers who are organized are far more likely to produce students who are organized. By modeling organization in the classroom, teachers can show the importance of taking care of school materials, following school routines, and having a place for everything in the classroom. All of these skills are easy to complete and cost very little to achieve in the classroom.

First, teachers need to be organized with materials in their classroom. By labeling homework trays, having a place to return materials, and teaching students to organize their own items, teachers will reinforce the importance of organization in the classroom. Also, little things like having all students write their names on papers and writing assignments in assignment notebooks can be helpful for both the organization of the teacher and the students.

Displaying a daily schedule of activities and assignments on the board or in a specific area is another great way to teach the skill of organization to children. Children will not only know the daily routine but will also see that teachers value the time spent in the classroom. By following a daily schedule as closely as possible, students will see that the teacher is organized and realize that time management is important in the skill of organization.

Allowing students to create learning contracts and complete projects is another way to teach organization in the classroom. Having older students create schedules and goals for learning will create a path for learning and see how organization is an important life skill as well. When students enter college, they typically receive a syllabus for learning and knowing how to plan and work ahead will be a helpful skill to know before they arrive at their college of choice.

Teachers can also encourage planning skills by helping students with personal organization such as writing down assignments in an assignment notebook or adding them to a calendar app in their cell phones. In addition, some students may need some extra assistance like writing down materials that are needed the next day or remembering an important school event. By helping students with this visual plan, they will show why organization is a vital skill in their lives.

Finally, modeling by thinking aloud is a great skill for teachers to use with their students. Planning a project or sharing about one's plans for the month are ways that teachers can model the skill of organization in their classrooms. Allowing students input into the real world of adults shows them that organization is an important skill for all ages.

While teachers are a crucial part of teaching organization for children, parents are usually the first people to teach children organization skills. From the time children are little they can begin to see that toys have their place, a routine happens at bedtime, and things go better when mom is on time and organized in the morning! The following section will explain how parents can teach the soft skill of organization to children.

HOW CAN PARENTS TEACH ORGANIZATION SKILLS TO CHILDREN?

Children begin learning organization skills far before they enter the classroom. They feel a sense of *normalcy* when things are running smoothly in their homes. They know what it is like on a regular morning versus a hurried one. While many parents know that a home should be clean and organized, they often don't realize how organization helps their children in other ways.

> If your child has organization issues opening her backpack can be a frightening experience. Crumpled assignments and tests, school announcements from two months ago, her missing house key—it's a mess! Many people think of organization skills as the ability to keep things in order. But people also use those skills to keep their thoughts in order so they can retrieve information and use it effectively. (Morin 2019)

As stated above, organization is much more than just the papers in a desk or backpack. Organization includes one's thought and actions as well. It is about being prepared for the day and having an organized mindset. While it can be frustrating to parents, the skill of organization for children is indeed important to their success. Developing these skills at an early age will follow children into adulthood and beyond. The following are ways that parents and families can help teach these skills at home.

To be organized, a child needs to first understand the importance of this skill. Expecting a kindergarten child to be organized on her own is most likely unattainable. Instead, parents need to explain that organization means knowing where your materials are, being prepared and ready for school each day, bringing home communication such as school notes and announcements, and being mentally organized as well.

Parents can teach organization by having a routine in place as much as possible. If children get home from school, have a snack, and get homework done before other activities, they can then put homework in their backpacks and be ready for the next day. Of course, this routine will not work every night, but sticking to it as much as possible will instill a sense of organization in children.

Practicing the motto *a place for everything and everything in its place* is also a great way to teach organization. If one teaches the skill of putting things back after they are used, children will be more likely to do this in the future. When toys are played with, putting them back in toy boxes or labeled crates will be helpful in both teaching the skill but also finding things the next time they are needed. When the scissors and school supplies are used, they need to go back in the drawer. Insisting on routine with materials works well with young students, but indeed may take some effort with teenagers!

Having a family calendar posted in a prominent place in the kitchen or family room is also helpful in teaching organization. As each member of the family receives schedules and dates, they can add to the family calendar. Encouraging children to be responsible for adding their own activities such as soccer practice, scouts, science fairs, and religious events can help them be organized in time and activities as well.

Older students with computers and cell phones can add activities to their calendars and notes sections to remind them of dates and plans for the future. Since this skill will be beneficial in college and careers, learning it as middle and high school students is helpful. Knowing how to organize activities and due dates is a great skill to have in the future. Any parent who has remembered soccer practice twenty minutes before they were to get children to the soccer field will also appreciate this effort by their families.

Parents can also teach organization by modeling it themselves. Thinking aloud about what they need to do tomorrow at work, writing lists for the grocery store, and planning carpool for the upcoming week show children how organization is helpful to adults as well. Even better, having children help with the grocery lists and activity planning are important life skills that they can use in the future. Children can help check for milk in the refrigerator, write the lists for the store, and help restock cabinets after the shopping is done. By doing activities that show organization, children will learn why organization is vital and will help their family as well.

Another activity that can help children with organization is laying one's clothes, backpacks, sports gear, and other needed items out the night before. Looking for the other shoe in the morning can mean missing the school bus, arriving late to school, and stress for both parents and children. However, if the clothes and supplies are laid out in the same place before going to bed, the idea of a calm morning is attainable.

In all, parents who model organization, follow through with clean up each night, and teach children to help with planning for activities and other family functions not only show the importance of this soft skill, but also save time and energy. Although it may take some time and effort in the beginning, if children are taught routines at an early age, they are far more likely to have these skills in place when they enter their first classrooms.

Overall, learning the soft skill of organization is an attribute that all people can benefit from. If parents and teachers work together, they can help children be prepared with materials, assignments, and other items that will help them be productive and they will model the importance of organization in the real world. Parents and teachers who help children with schedules and outside activities are also teaching the importance of time management in the organization process.

By teaching children organization and the idea that everything has its place, both parents and teachers will enable students to be responsible and will be far less likely to lose items in the process. Quick tasks like labeling and putting materials away after use seem simple but are practical strategies in the area of organization. Another area that requires organization is that of learning in an online setting. Teaching children the skill of organization will help them learn important strategies for learning online. The next section will address how to teach this soft skill in a virtual environment.

HOW DO KIDS LEARN ORGANIZATION IN AN ONLINE SETTING?

As stated above, organization is an important skill both at school and at home. However, it is even more important when learning in a virtual environment. Students who are learning online need to be prepared and organized for the day and be able to access materials and supplies in order to learn efficiently in an online setting. Having the materials needed for the school day will

eliminate stress and enable students to learn efficiently and without the interruption of looking for items while trying to participate in online classes.

One of the first things that a teacher can do to help with organization in an
online setting is to communicate with parents and families about what will be
needed for lessons. For example, if the students need a calculator for a math
assignment or a box of crayons for a kindergarten science lesson, teachers
need to provide of list of these materials *in advance* to parents. While some
schools provided materials to students who are learning online, making sure
that basic school supplies and items from around the house are available is
important to happen before lessons begin. Ensuring that students are prepared
and ready for lessons by providing families with either the needed materials
or a list of the materials from home is a vital part of learning to be organized
online. If students are unprepared and looking for pencils in the middle of
the lesson, they will lose much of the content and explanation that is given
during this lost time.

Teachers can also make sure that students have a schedule of the school day
that is both accurate and shared with parents and students. Log in times, free
time, lunch, and other items need to be prepared in advance, as a schedule
of the day's learning is important to help children be both organized and less
stressed in an online environment. For older students, knowing when each
class period starts and ends, the procedures for logging in and attendance,
and the protocol for classes like study hall and physical education are also
important to announce and expect during the virtual school day.

Parents can help with organization by preparing a learning area for the children in the household. Arranging for a desk or table for writing, an internet
connection and charging cord for computer assistance, and supplies and materials for learning are all important for children to be successful in an online
environment. Working in conjunction with the school and teacher, making
sure that the supplies and items needed for lessons are available, and having
a place assigned for learning will all be helpful. Also, finding a place that is
free from distractions such as television will help students to concentrate on
their work without the temptation of other distractions in the room.

Another way that parents can help with organization is by helping their
children with schedules, lunch breaks, and other parts of the school day.
Young children who are not capable of telling time yet may need extra guidance with this part of organization during the school day.

Finally, parents can help with organization by checking off homework,
reading logs, and other items that will be required in an online environment.
Helping children create a To Do list of the projects and assignments that are
due will help children learn this skill for the future. High school students will
most likely be more independent in this area, but a check in to see how things
are going is still helpful, especially if your child is typically disorganized or

a procrastinator. Knowing in advance how children learn and what they need most in the area of organization will help parents do a nightly check to make sure that students are both on target and ready for the next virtual school day.

Taking the time to teach organization to children is a skill that will benefit everyone. Parents will be far less stressed in the mornings, teachers will have classrooms that look organized and neat in appearance, and future employers will have workers who understand the importance of this skill. Teaching this skill in an online setting, where organization and independence are crucial, will also benefit both young children and high school students. Being prepared with organization skills will make the world a better place for students of the future.

KEY IDEAS

- Organization skills are needed by people of all ages.
- Children who lack organization skills often lose assignments and forget due dates.
- Organization skills directly impact one's success in the classroom, regardless of the educational setting.
- Organization is a soft skill that can be taught and nurtured.
- Parents and teachers should work together to practice organization skills that will help children in their learning, whether in a traditional classroom setting or a virtual classroom.
- Children who learn organization skills at an early age will take this soft skill into their future college and career options.

Chapter 12

Time Management

Why is time management an important skill for kids?
How can educators teach the skill of time management to students?
How can parents teach the skill of time management to children?
How can kids learn time management in an online setting?

IMPORTANCE OF TIME MANAGEMENT

Time management is a soft skill that can be used by children as well as adults. Being on time for classes and meetings, being aware of time and space, and using time in a productive manner are all important for children to learn. Time management also impacts one's ability to organize and prioritize items that must be done on a daily basis.

In a recent edition of *Psychology Today*, Eileen Kennedy-Moore (2014) stated, "Understanding time helps kids to use their time well. It's a key part of executive functioning skills such as planning and prioritizing."

Being aware of time and how it works is a basic skill that all children need. From the time a child is little, being aware of schedules like breakfast in the morning, lunch at midday, and dinner in the evening are some of the first time-oriented events that children learn. Also, the sequencing of events in the day helps children learn that routine can be a helpful way to stay organized and on top of things.

Time management is especially helpful as children reach school age and begin to learn that *there is only so much time in a day.* By learning to effectively use time and schedules, school-age children will be able to develop the skill of time management that they will use for the rest of their lives. Regardless of the career path that one eventually chooses, being on time and using this valuable resource efficiently will help children be better prepared for the future.

Time management helps with organization, planning, scheduling, and many other elements that help both children and adults. Being able to manage one's time can help prepare students for the future and will enable them to see the importance of making the most of every minute of their day.

There are many ways that both teachers and parents can help children learn the skill of time management. Being able to create and follow schedules, work under time demands, and use time efficiently are all ways that adults can help children learn this skill. The following are ways that educators can teach and model this skill for children.

HOW CAN EDUCATORS TEACH TIME MANAGEMENT TO CHILDREN?

Teachers are important in teaching and modeling the skill of time management for children. In most elementary schools, a schedule of subjects, lunch, and recess are dictated by the administration. Teachers who follow these schedules model the soft skill of time management to their students. If they are prompt and on time, the students will see the importance of following schedules, and the other school faculty who are involved (such as cafeteria workers and special area teachers) will appreciate that their schedules are not hindered by the tardiness of others.

Students in junior high and high school are often penalized for arriving *after the bell*, so learning time management at an early age will help them as well. Teachers in the upper grades who follow bell schedules and begin each new class promptly model that their teaching time is important and that the learning time of students is valued.

Teachers can also model time management by creating a homework schedule. Having certain items done on a routine schedule can help both parents and children plan for the assignments that are expected each week. Providing a schedule to parents that is consistent and familiar can help families plan for the week and ensure that homework is completed each evening. For example, if students study math facts on Mondays, do reading on Tuesdays, etc. parents will know what to expect and can help their children plan their time accordingly.

For older students, assigning a project that is done in stages and has a calendar for completion can help students learn time management. If a completed project is due in two weeks, giving the students checkpoints along the way will benefit students who tend to procrastinate. Having the project outline due on day 2, a model due on day 4, and steps of the research outlined for the rest of the project will help children learn to manage their time and will help teachers stay organized as well.

As students prepare for high school and college, teaching them about scheduling and study time is also a useful life skill. Teaching students how to read and use a class syllabus, plan for projects and assignments, and create a dedicated study time are useful to students but are rarely taught as required study skills in today's classrooms. Teachers who take the time to do this will create students who understand the importance of schedules, timelines, and due dates, all tools that are needed for today's scholars.

Creating a homework folder, assignment notebook, and family communication plan can also help teachers instruct students about time management. Sometimes a visual such as a calendar or checklist can help children see what is due, what is completed, and what still needs to be completed. Sending this information home on a daily or weekly basis also creates a routine that both children and parents appreciate. Teachers who hand out random assignments, expect projects that are not given the ample time to complete, and do not provide feedback in an appropriate amount of time can cause stress for students.

By creating homework folders and assignment notebooks, children can practice time management and learn this skill at a very young age. Older students who use class calendars and syllabi will practice using the time management that will be needed for both college and career readiness.

On a final note, teaching children to sometimes take a break from schoolwork is also important. Just like adults who have coffee breaks, lunch schedules, and a short time for relaxing between activities, children need the same unscheduled time in their day. When teachers notice that children are bored or overwhelmed with the content of a lesson, taking a *brain break* can be very effective. According to UNICEF (2019):

> Brain Breaks for kids is the simple technique in which young students are given a short mental break taken at regular intervals. Most brain breaks range from around 5 to 20 minutes as a general rule, although most people prefer to keep them short and on point. For maximum success, it's usually best to include a physical activity that will compliment mental energy.

Brain breaks work for all children from preschool to high school age. Sometimes, simply taking a short break from academics can renew and refresh both the mind and the body and allow students time to redirect and refocus after a quick but valuable activity. Even though this takes a few minutes from the schedule, the productivity which follows a brain break can be remarkable.

One other break that will help children is the idea of recess. Recess, a time for unstructured play, allows students a break from academics and encourages free play and physical exercise. While many schools are decreasing or even eliminating recess from school schedules, researchers at Harvard Health

(2019) found that "The loss of unstructured time for students may not be achieving its aims. Students who are kept in classrooms all day without a break are likely to be less attentive and may also learn less efficiently."

While teaching children to properly manage their time, learn organization of projects, and work within schedules in a school setting, learning to take the time to just relax and play is also an important part of time management. As adults know that taking a walk, having a coffee break, and stretching for a minute can help them get back on task, students need to learn that a quick break can benefit one's time on task as well.

In conclusion, teachers play an important role in teaching children about time management. By teaching the importance of following schedules, using planning strategies, and helping with routines and schedules, educators can help children with this important skill. On the same note, teaching children to take breaks and refocus is also a vital part of learning time management in the classroom.

The next section will discuss ways that parents can help children learn time management in the home setting. Though the tasks required at school and home are different, the skill of time management is one that will carry over into multiple settings.

HOW CAN PARENTS TEACH TIME MANAGEMENT TO CHILDREN?

Parents are busy people. There are jobs to do, chores to attend to, and dinner to prepare. Keeping the family in a routine and schedule is often hard to do, with so much going on both in and out of the home. However, parents who model the skill of time management and teach children about being prepared and ready will raise children who do the same.

Very early in a child's life he/she can begin learning about time management. Beginning with concepts like morning and evening or wake up and night time, children can learn that very specific things happen during these hours. Developing a schedule that one follows in the morning and at bedtime are ways that a young child can learn about using time efficiently and teaches the concept of sequencing as well. Doing a routine in order each night that includes brushing teeth, getting a drink, and reading a story is a great way to begin teaching time management to young children.

As children get older, creating a schedule, either in pictures or words, can help them put their mornings together. Some parents even create a checklist that helps children remember the steps of getting ready for school. Those who have children who are not *morning people* may find this especially helpful in getting out the door in the mornings!

Along with time management for routines, laying out clothes for the next morning, having lunches packed and in the refrigerator, and backpacks ready to go can also help the morning routines go smoother and quicker. By teaching about the elements of routine and organization, children can learn that by being organized and ready, they will also have more time to get things done.

Homework is often a stressful time for families. However, creating a routine for homework can also be helpful to school-age children. Allowing children a few minutes of *down time* to just decompress and relax, followed by a healthy snack is a great way to ease into the homework challenge. Then, after a set time (usually an hour or less), children should begin homework and get it finished before being allowed video games or TV time. By having a set homework schedule each afternoon/evening, children are more apt to complete homework and are less likely to be stressed about its completion.

For older children, keeping a homework notebook that is written in each day is a very helpful tool for both home and school. As children complete the homework each evening, they can check off the items and know that the items are finished and ready to turn in the next morning. For busy children who know ahead of time that they have a soccer game during the week, encouraging them to work ahead on projects and assignments can also help alleviate last minute stress and anxiety—for both children and parents.

Creating a schedule both for the individual child and the family can also help with the soft skill of time management. Some families create a color-coded calendar in which all of the family events are planned and coordinated. With each member of the family receiving their own unique color it is easy to see at a glance the schedule for the week. By displaying a calendar on the refrigerator or a common area in the house, parents can model how to plan for the week, and children can see where they spend the majority of their time.

Parents who see that their children are overscheduled and stressed can also point out how many activities a child is doing and suggest that maybe they cut down on activities or reallocate their time. While this may not be easy to do simply in conversation, sometimes a visual of the week can represent just where time is being spent. Prioritizing events and activities by importance and interest can help children use their time more wisely and effectively.

On another note, using the soft skill of time management is one that is also needed in an online environment. By learning some basic strategies for managing one's time, this can be used in online classes as well. The following section will provide some ideas for how to do this.

HOW CAN KIDS LEARN TIME MANAGEMENT
IN AN ONLINE SETTING?

Students learning in an online setting often struggle with the skill of time management. While teachers may do their best to organize the virtual classroom and provide schedules and calendars, it is ultimately up to the student to log into classes and complete assignments. Younger children will obviously need some assistance in this area, but junior high and high school students should be capable of logging on at the correct time, and participating in classes as required.

Teachers can help teach the skill of time management in an online environment by providing a schedule of classes and subjects. For younger children these could even be visual with pictures and clocks to model the subjects and timeframes for students. For older students, the school will provide a daily schedule that explains the times and teachers for each course. Regardless of the grade level, making sure that students understand the time schedule as well as expectations will be helpful on the part of the teacher.

Teachers can also help with online time management by providing time for group work, projects, recess, and other important areas of the day. If students need to complete group projects, for example, providing time during the day for breakout rooms, working on a Google Doc, or another group activity is indeed appreciated by students. Providing this time during the class, rather than expecting the students to complete projects after school should ensure that the project is completed and that the teacher is checking in on the progress on a daily basis.

Just like the advice of breaking projects into smaller steps and checking in on the progress that was mentioned earlier, this tool also is helpful in an online environment. The more that a teacher can do to provide guidance, help break work into manageable chunks, and provide feedback along the way, the more successful the students will be both in time management and the project as well.

Parents can also help students learn time management in an online setting. Providing the necessary tools such as a clock, calendar, and planner will all assist students in become more adept at time management. Also, checking in on children to see how they are doing, making sure that due dates are being met and assignments are being turned in, is also a strategy that parents can do at home.

Even though kids may be learning in an online environment, they will also have other activities and commitments to take care of during virtual learning. Helping children plan for these activities and how they will interact with homework and family time is also an important discussion that parents can help children learn. Sharing one's own plan for managing their time for the day at work and at home is also a nice idea for parents who are helping with this skill at home. Many parents are now working virtually from home, and modeling how to do this without the boss checking in will enable students to see why time management and a self-driven schedule are helpful in a grown up world as well.

In brief, learning the skill of time management is a tool that can help children far into the future. Time management is not just used by young children, but helps as college students begin managing course schedules, and adult workers complete projects in a timely manner. Being able to manage one's time at school, at home, and while learning virtually is something that will assist students and will be a valuable skill in the future.

KEY IDEAS

- Time management is a skill that begins with very young children as they learn a sense of time and routine.
- Parents can help children learn time management by creating schedules and routines in the mornings, for homework, and at bedtime.
- Creating family schedules can help with time management and help make activities less stressful.
- Teachers can help students learn time management skills by adhering to schedules and teaching about the impact of timeliness on learning, whether at school or in an online setting.
- Teachers can also help students learn time management in the creation of homework schedules and project checkpoints.
- Learning time management as well as when to take a break and refocus are skills that children will use for a lifetime.

Chapter 13

Balance

Why is the skill of balance important to kids?
How can educators teach balance to students?
How can parents teach balance to children?
How can kids learn balance in an online setting?

IMPORTANCE OF BALANCE

According to the Oxford Dictionary (2019), the word balance means "an even distribution of weight enabling someone or something to remain upright and steady. Mental or emotional stability. The way to some kind of peace and personal balance." While one normally thinks of balance in terms of standing on one foot without falling over, it also applies to having everything in one's life balanced as well.

In terms of children, balance means having activities, schoolwork, and other needs in place so that one does not lose control. It means that a child is involved and busy, without being overcommitted. Children who are balanced can participate in extracurricular activities, enjoy school, and have family time without feeling stressed or overwhelmed.

In the classic book *The Hurried Child* by David Elkind (1981) the author pointed out that children are experiencing more stress than necessary and are being forced into the role of *miniature adults*. By adding pressure and stress to the lives of children they often do not learn to attain balance in their lives and relationships. This book was a pinnacle in pointing out the need for balance in children.

Another way that balance has been defined in the lives of children is through the *Sandwich Analogy*. According to Stauffenger (2019), a mental sandwich for children should include "Part work, part play, part serious thinking, and part restful enjoyment . . . Because of the breadth of those four pieces, all that your kids' lives include are in there. You will be able to instantly see what is out of balance."

The sandwich model is a great way of showing children how balance is important in their daily lives. If their entire day is consumed with school and homework, or sports activities, with little time to do other things, they will likely become tired, overwhelmed, and even stressed. Teaching children the important aspects of balancing the time and activities in their lives is an important soft skill that will take them into adulthood.

For children today, many opportunities are present through school, sports leagues, faith-based organizations, and others. Encouraging them to participate and be active in such organizations is important to both social and emotional needs. However, how does one participate and be happy, without becoming overcommitted and overly stressed? The following section will address the soft skill of balance and how teachers can help develop this skill in children.

HOW CAN EDUCATORS TEACH BALANCE TO CHILDREN?

Teachers play an important role in the balance of children. Just like they balance the school day with just the right amount of active learning and quiet learning, a teacher can play a huge role in creating a balanced lifestyle for his/her students.

One of the first things that comes to mind when thinking of how schools are a part of a balanced child is that of homework. While homework can have healthy benefits of having the child review and apply new curriculum, too much of it can be overwhelming to children. According to the National Education Association "Research Spotlight on Homework" (2019):

> The National PTA recommendations fall in line with general guidelines and suggest 10–20 minutes per night in the first grade, and an additional 10 minutes per grade level thereafter (e.g., 20 minutes for second grade, 120 minutes for twelfth). High school students may sometimes do more, depending on what classes they take.

Teachers who assign homework within these guidelines will model the idea that homework is important, but also that this is not the only thing that children should be doing in the evening. Teachers who promote family activities, reading at bedtime, and playing outside will produce children who are well rounded and not overwhelmed with hours of homework each night.

Another idea for teaching balance in the school day is by using this technique in lesson planning and curriculum for one's teaching. Creating a balance of project-based learning with pencil and paper work will help students see balance in the school day. Also, doing differing activities throughout the day such as a balance of group and individual work will also teach and model that children learn in a variety of ways, and that different approaches will help reach the needs of all students in the classroom.

For older students, the idea of contracts or syllabi are helpful in creating balanced students. When introducing a new project, for example, a teacher can model an appropriate timeline for completing the daily activities which lead up to the final product. By modeling how to pace one's learning, complete projects in small *chunks,* and plan for each part on a daily basis, they can show children how to balance their time and energy in the school setting. Creating a contract for learning with an estimated timeline for each step of the project is a visual way for students to see their progress as well as what still needs to be completed.

Homework binders or home/school communication folders are also a great way to share information with parents and families. By having a communication system in place with homework for the week and announcements about school activities and other events, parents will be able to help children balance their home and school lives.

For older students, a syllabus for the class with due dates, projects, and tests on it will help them balance their school and home lives. If a child has a family function, teaching them to work ahead can benefit them in terms of time management and stress reduction. This is also a great skill for students to have as they approach college and career readiness, as a balanced workload will prevent cramming for tests, having all night study sessions, and panicking at the last minute when projects are not completed.

Working with a school counselor on presentations for students is another great way to build balance in children. School counselors or other mental health professionals can create short lessons on how to balance home and school, when activities are just too much, and how to prioritize the events in a child's life. Sharing examples of a child who is doing too much can be a great way to model this soft skill for children.

Finally, a teacher who shares about his/her own balancing act can have a huge impact on students. Thinking aloud with comments like, "Wow. I have a lot on my plate this week, with all of those projects to grade and a baseball game for my son. However, I know that I can grade a bit each night and get all of it done," can show students that adults have to balance things as well. As long as the teacher is not complaining about the workload, sharing the idea of balance with children is important.

Also sharing how the teacher does things for fun can model the idea of balance in the classroom. Sharing a few personal stories like how the teacher participates in family events, a yoga class for relaxation, or a book club for outside reading can model the idea of taking care of oneself outside the classroom and promotes a healthy view of a working adult who has a balanced life.

In conclusion, teachers can do a great deal to help children learn the soft skill of balance. By learning to have an even amount of outside activities, family time, schoolwork, and play time, children will be able to attain balance in their lives. Working together to make sure that children are not over-scheduled or overcommitted, teachers and parents can help develop the whole child, and one who is happy and healthy, instead of overwhelmed and stressed. The following section focuses on strategies that can be taught in the home.

HOW CAN PARENTS TEACH BALANCE TO CHILDREN?

Many opportunities exist for children to be active and participate with friends in activities and adventures. Being able to be a part of a group or organization is important in the development of self-esteem and social skills. Children naturally want to explore new adventures, have fun with friends, and be active and busy. However, at what point do parents say that enough is enough?

The idea of balance in children is one that involves making sure that children have a healthy proportion of home, school, and outside activities, while maintaining a level of harmony and happiness. It means that a child can be home for Sunday dinner with the family, keep homework and grades in check, while still enjoying outside activities with friends.

Modeling balance by parents and caregivers is a great way to practice balance in the home. If children see parents who work every night, run from one activity to the next, and are overcommitted themselves, they are likely to model this as well. While leaving that stack of papers at work or calling a client from the office instead of home may be challenging for parents, it is important that children see them having down time as well.

Parents can help to achieve a balance in their children's lives in various ways. First, it is important to examine the personal family values and time constraints that exist in the lives of their children. One quick and easy way to determine this is by looking at the family calendar and deciding which activities are most important and which are the most time consuming.

Designing a calendar which lists all of the activities of each person in the family can help show how busy or scheduled a child is in the household. If the child is scheduled for an event or activity every day of the week, parents should ask if this is too much, and if the children have time to relax, do healthy outdoor activities, and simply have *down time* for relaxing with family and friends.

Along with this is the idea of allowing some time in the week where the children have no commitments, activities, or events to attend. Having unplanned *play time* in the week is a great way to make sure that kids are unplugged, active, and able to just enjoy time with friends and family. Having a Fun Friday or a Sibling Saturday allows children to interact with others without having to be at a prearranged activity.

Limiting activities to just one sport, one faith-based activity, and one school or club activity is another great way to achieve balance. While students may want to participate in every activity and sport that a school offers, learning to make choices and prioritize time commitments can lead to a more balanced lifestyle for children. Doing just one sport per season, one activity at school, and one outside activity, children will see that these commitments take time, energy, and devotion to make them all work.

Considering the age and developmental level of the child is also important in these choices. Younger children may need to start with just one activity and grow into others as they are more responsible and better at managing time. Parents will know when to add on these activities by watching how committed and interested their children are in doing them.

Another idea on the balance of activities and commitments for children has to do with interest and enjoyment. Often times, children *think* they would like to try a new sport or club yet find out rather quickly that it isn't for them. Having a family rule that children must finish what they start is a great way for children to learn the idea of commitment to a team or a project. Finishing the baseball season, for example, shows that one is a good teammate, and a dedicated person. Not signing up for the *next* season, however, is always an option!

Finally, parents need to step back and take a look at the reasons their children are involved in the activities and commitments that they are. Does she truly enjoy dance class? Does he cry at every soccer practice? On the ride home, does the child share the awesome things that happened in the club or complain about what happened or threaten to quit? Watching and listening to children is a great way to know if the children are indeed interested and willing, or simply going through the motions of the activity involved.

Parents have a lot on their plates and balancing a family schedule can take a great deal of planning and execution. However, making sure that children have time for family, schoolwork, play, and rest is an important part in the development of children. Learning to prioritize, look at the daily schedule, and have time to just be kids is an important part of being a child today.

Learning about balance in an online environment is important in developing this soft skill as well. Balancing one's responsibilities in an online learning environment is important for a successful experience. The next section will explain how to do this in virtual classes.

HOW CAN KIDS LEARN BALANCE IN AN ONLINE SETTING?

Balancing one's schoolwork and one's personal schedule can be challenging for children and young adults to do. Adding the additional realm of online learning can make this even more difficult. However, by working together teachers and parents can help students learn the skill of balance in a way that will help them most.

In an ordinary classroom setting, teachers are constantly monitoring students. They roam the classroom looking for students who are off task, did not complete last night's homework, or even those who may appear sick or tired. However, in an online learning environment this may be a bit more difficult to do. Therefore, both teachers and parents need to share this responsibility, especially with younger students.

Teachers can help children learn balance in an online setting by doing frequent check-ins with students. Having a morning meeting to check on the wellness of students, as well as the stress levels and workloads that children are dealing with each day is important. Even in a virtual setting, teachers will be able to pick up on students who are trying to do too much, or are not receiving enough sleep each night. Checking in with parents to make sure that the lessons and homework are manageable is important as well. Touching base and doing check-ins between parents and teachers is an excellent idea for virtual learning, as it allows both parties to make sure that the children are learning the appropriate materials without being overwhelmed.

When students are learning in a virtual setting, it is tempting for families to enroll their children in many extracurricular activities to make up for the reduced social time that happens online. However, remembering to still maintain a balance between outside activities and schoolwork is indeed an important issue to consider. Just like the suggestions listed in the home school connections above, making sure that students are not overscheduled is important to their well-being.

Parents can also help with the skill of balance by encouraging students to take scheduled breaks, eat a healthy snack or lunch, and playing outside, even for a few minutes, during the school day. Taking breaks and getting some fresh air will help students focus and show more attention in the online environment. By checking in to make sure that these breaks are indeed being taken by students, parents can help provide more balance during the school day.

By working together, teachers and parents can help children learn the soft skill of balance. Learning this skill at a young age, while making sure to cover the requirements of school, the responsibilities of home, and the time for personal well-being, is a vital part of using balance in college and careers. Learning to balance one's life will help children be both successful students and well-rounded individuals in their very busy lives.

KEY POINTS

- Balance is the idea of planning one's activities and responsibilities in a way that is not overwhelming to children.
- Teachers can help with balance in the classroom or during virtual learning by arranging content and curriculum appropriately.
- Teachers can also help with balance by providing appropriate homework that is respectful but not overwhelming.
- Balance also includes unplanned time and down time for children as well as families. Breaks during online learning are also important to remember.
- Parents can help children learn balance by examining and prioritizing activities and creating a calendar as a visual of these items.
- Learning the skill of balance will help prepare children for both college and career experiences.

Chapter 14

Positive Attitude

Why is a positive attitude important to kids?
How can educators teach about a positive attitude to students?
How can parents teach about a positive attitude to children?
How can kids learn a positive attitude in an online setting?

WHY IS A POSITIVE ATTITUDE
IMPORTANT TO CHILDREN?

A positive attitude is one of the most important things we can teach our children. Learning to look for the best in life, turning a bad day into a good one, and having a great outlook on life can help children be successful both in school and in the future. People who are negative and only look for the bad are often stressed, overwhelmed, and prone to more illness. Negative attitudes can impact everything that one does and can create environments of negativity in all areas of one's life.

A positive attitude, on the other hand, can promote positivity, wellness, and a healthy outlook. Being positive is an attribute that helps in the home, school, and office setting. It is a skill that children need to be successful, both in school and in future careers. Employers appreciate a positive attitude in the workplace and people generally like to be around those with a positive attitude more than a negative one.

Teaching children to be positive is a soft skill that parents and educators can both teach and model for the children around them. By creating positive environments, having an optimistic outlook, and looking for the best in life, they show children from very early stages that a positive outlook can take you far. Parents and teachers who show children how to take a bad day and make it better model for children that one bad incident in the day does not have to ruin it.

In today's world, children are facing more pressure, stress, and life changes than ever before. Learning to be hopeful and positive can help make life more manageable and is a skill that can be used forever. According to Ripa Ajmera of LiveStrong.com (2019):

> In a world filled with negativity, violence and suffering, a positive attitude can make life more manageable. Although it's impossible to fully control life events, you can control your reactions to what happens. This attitude enables you to develop the strength to deal with life's challenges. When children develop a positive attitude early in life, positive thinking becomes a habit that can ease the pressures associated with growing up.

The power of *positive thinking* can be taught in many different ways, both at school and home. By practicing a few simple things each day, both teachers and parents can teach this soft skill to children. The next section will explain how teachers can teach and model this skill in the classroom.

HOW CAN EDUCATORS TEACH ABOUT A POSITIVE ATTITUDE TO CHILDREN?

There are a variety of ways that educators can teach and model a positive attitude in the classroom. The first begins with a positive outlook and nurturing environment in the classroom. A teacher who is kind and welcoming every day, leaves personal problems at home, and creates a classroom that is community oriented is modeling a positive outlook to the class. Even though changes in the schedule happen, a child acts out, or a bad thing happens, teachers need to remain positive to the best of their abilities.

Beginning each day as a new day—regardless of what happened in the past—is a great way to model positivity in the classroom. Teachers who hold grudges, bring personal problems into the classroom, or model negative behavior are likely to create students who act the same. Children look up to teachers and watch as they handle both the good and bad things that happen during the day. Teachers who can work through the negative are modeling this disposition to the children in their classroom.

Teachers can also create positive classroom environments by teaching about an affirming mindset in the classroom. A positive or growth mindset implies that the intelligence and outlook of children can be encouraged through attitude and effort in the classroom. Teachers who instruct children about the importance of believing in themselves, putting forth effort in the classroom, and working toward accomplishments can assist students in learning how to be positive. Recent research by the Education Week Research Center (2016) indicated that:

> Teachers overwhelmingly agree that incorporating growth mindset into their practice could have significant effects for student learning and the quality of instruction. Nearly all of the teachers surveyed (98%) agreed that integrating the concept of students' growth mindset into their classroom practice will improve student learning (26).

Along with a growth mindset in the classroom, teachers can also help with positive attitudes by having children set attainable goals and encouraging them to be successful. Teachers who allow children to set goals, help them achieve, and celebrate their successes will enable children to grow and learn about the idea of being positive. When children see that they can indeed learn and achieve their goals they are apt to be more positive about the next obstacle before them.

Teachers can also assist students in developing a positive attitude by placing an emphasis on encouraging words and phrases in the classroom. Creating a positive class motto, decorating the classroom with children's work and successes, and providing positive quotes and posters is another great way to create positivity. Inspirational and encouraging quotes in the classroom surround children with the positive energy they need to succeed.

Quotabulary.com (2018), a website which contains encouraging passages and quotations, states the following:

> Words which spread hope and influence the process of thinking in a positive manner are required for the purpose of motivation and the healthy growth of kids. Positive and encouraging quotes for kids . . . should act as a source of positive energy and shape the mind of kids.

By creating a positive environment, sharing encouraging words, and displaying optimistic quotes, teachers will model the idea of positivity and will show this belief to students and anyone else who enters the classroom. Since a positive attitude can be contagious, seeing such displays around them will encourage students to share this disposition with others.

Teachers can also promote the idea of positivity in the classroom by using praise and encouragement with students. While all children will not do well on assignments or tests, providing praise for what they did correctly and encouraging them to do better the next time can go a long way in the classroom. By providing positive feedback to students, teachers can model the value of working hard, trying one's best, and remaining positive about the next task which students must attempt.

Community Circles or Morning Meetings are also excellent ways of creating positivity in the classroom and setting the tone for the day. By assembling the students for a quick Morning Meeting to talk about events for the day, discuss concerns from the children, and establish a positive rapport for the learning, teachers will create an environment of caring and nurturing. Listening to children and allowing them input into issues of the school or classroom encourages students that they have the power to make changes and the ability to be heard.

Using bibliotherapy, or the idea of reading a book with a particular purpose, is another way that teachers can instruct about a positive attitude in the classroom. Reading about a character who has a problem, is in an adverse situation, or is feeling sad can display to children how to learn from problems, and turn them into something more positive. Sometimes, reading about a character with a similar problem can help children learn that they are not alone in what they are dealing with.

Talking about real-life people in the world who are inspirational and demonstrate a positive attitude is another way to teach about this skill in the classroom. There are people all around us who model a positive attitude, have overcome a difficult situation, or rise to the top—despite difficult circumstances. Talking about these people, whether they are in the local community, or in the national news, is a beneficial way for students to see that a positive attitude can help one with even the most difficult problems.

In summary, teachers need to model and teach the importance of a positive attitude in the classroom. By creating an environment which focuses on positivity, is student oriented, and focuses on community, students will have a place where they can share problems, make mistakes, and learn to be positive in difficult situations. Using community circles, displaying positive quotes, and involving students in decision-making can also be useful in creating the nurturing environments in which children will thrive. Regardless of the strategies the teacher uses, modeling the idea of a positive attitude is the most important one they can choose.

Parents, too, are an important part of teaching about a positive attitude to children. The following section explores ideas for teaching and modeling this skill at home.

HOW CAN PARENTS TEACH ABOUT A POSITIVE ATTITUDE TO CHILDREN?

A positive attitude begins in the home, from the minute a child arrives. It involves being nurturing and confident in communicating with children and keeping a great attitude toward life. A positive attitude means working through the bad things that happen and continuing to be positive despite them. Although raising children can be an incredibly difficult and stressful experience, it is also one of the greatest joys that parents can have.

Modeling positive parenting through positive discipline, teamwork, and an encouraging environment will help children maintain an upbeat attitude that will help them in all areas of their schooling and future careers. By beginning the process with a positive home environment, parents can model this for their children.

According to Gallegos (2019) from the Center for Parenting Education, "You can start by encouraging positive thinking and by creating an environment that nurtures your children's beliefs in their abilities. Having that confidence enables them to take risks that will help them reach their potential." By believing in the abilities of children and providing encouragement and support for them, parents begin the journey of teaching a positive mindset to their families.

Modeling and talking about how parents work through tough times is a great way to show children how to create a positive environment in their own lives. All parents have rough days, whether it is at home when an appliance breaks, or at work when one deals with a difficult co-worker or a problem on a work-related project. However, showing children that it's not *the end of the world* can make a huge difference.

Sharing what caused the problem and how one plans to deal with it is beneficial to both parents and children. By thinking through the problem and brainstorming solutions together, parents will be able to determine resolutions, but will also model this skill for children. Handling problems in a calm manner can show them that even the worst problems can be turned into positive situations.

Parents can also teach a positive attitude by helping children with their own problems or concerns. If a child is worried about a confrontation with a friend or an upcoming test, parents can help children develop some possible solutions, share stories about similar events when they were younger, and learn that a positive outlook can help more than anything. Sometimes, an empathetic listener and encourager is all that a child needs to come up with his/her own solutions. Hopefully, by doing this, children will learn to turn the problem into a positive outcome.

In brief, children need to see a positive attitude modeled by the people in their lives. If they wake up each morning to a grumpy environment, they are apt to model this in their own lives. Seeing and living in a home of positivity can make a huge impact on school and future successes.

A positive attitude in an online setting is also an important part of learning for today's students. The next section will explain ways that both teachers and parents can help kids learn this skill in a virtual environment.

HOW CAN KIDS LEARN A POSITIVE
ATTITUDE IN AN ONLINE SETTING?

Learning in an online setting can be a very different experience for children. The logistics of online classes, the lack of friends and classmates sitting next to you, and the independence level that is required of students can be a lot for young people to deal with. However, creating a positive learning environment and learning a positive attitude can be one of the most important skills in this area.

Teachers can help with developing positive attitudes by creating a positive learning environment in an online class. Getting to know the students, taking the time to build relationships, and having a personal approach to teaching is a great start. Starting the morning with Community Circles and Morning Meetings to check in on concerns and worries is also helpful in creating positivity each day. Even though it is tempting to lecture to students in this learning format, remembering to create an atmosphere of fun and hands-on learning is especially important in virtual settings. Students who have fun activities are far more likely to be engaged and active than in an environment that consists of worksheets and lectures.

Teachers can also model positive attitudes in their own instruction. On the days that the internet does not cooperate, the video does not load, and the video conference is lagging, it is important to maintain composure and positivity in the classroom. Technology will have problems and a backup plan for these issues as well as a "go with the flow attitude" will be helpful to not only the students but the teacher as well. Remembering to practice grace and forgiveness in an online environment is vital for teachers who may not have been prepared for the virtual environments that they are now teaching in. Also, a teacher who can laugh with and enjoy the students is one who will create positive attitudes in a virtual classroom as well.

Parents can help with a positive attitude with students who are learning online as well. Being prepared for the learning and greeting each day with a smile will help kids do the same. While in traditional learning, parents are responsible for getting kids dressed and out the door, parents are now typically at home and responsible for the online learning. Remembering to model a positive attitude, avoiding critical comments about teachers, and providing help and reassurance to children can be one of the most important parts of developing this skill while students learn virtually. Technology will have problems and things may not go perfectly, but being able to smile and model positivity is a vital part of helping children learn this skill.

Overall, learning in an online setting presents its own challenges and concerns. Not being with classmates in a typical classroom, having to navigate the technology required in virtual learning, and not having a teacher who is physically present can be overwhelming to children! Teaching students who are far away and creating lessons virtually is challenging to educators, and having one's home suddenly become a school can be demanding for parents and families. Remembering to create a positive environment for learning and modeling positivity and encouragement to children is one of the most important things that adults can do. By working together to teach the soft skill of a positive attitude, children will be prepared for the future of college and job settings where positivity will be key.

KEY IDEAS

- Children need positive environments both at home and at school.
- Providing encouragement and modeling a positive attitude are important for both parents and teachers to do. Working together on this skill, whether at school or online, is vital to promote this skill in children.
- Teachers can help children learn positive attitudes by using a growth mindset and setting attainable goals with the students.
- Morning Meetings and Community Circles are great ways to set the tone for the day in the classroom and promote a positive classroom environment, even in an online environment.
- Parents can assist children in developing a positive attitude by sharing their own problems and modeling how they were solved.
- Teaching and modeling the soft skill of a positive attitude are lifelong skills that all children need.

Conclusion

Why do soft skills matter to kids?
How do soft skills apply to teachers?
Why do soft skills matter to parents?
How will soft skills help in the future of online teaching?
What are the next steps in teaching soft skills to children?

WHY DO SOFT SKILLS MATTER?

Soft Skills for Kids was written as a guide for teachers and parents who want to help their children be prepared for the world of challenges, adversity, and problems they may face. However, it was also written to prepare students for the successes, accomplishments, and feats that they will encounter as well. Soft skills are about creating children who are well rounded, prepared, and ready for the future ahead of them. The book was also recently revised to include new ideas for both teaching and learning online, as soft skills are important in this environment as well.

Soft skills are skills that will prepare young children for working together in the family unit. Yes, two year olds will still throw tantrums on occasion, and siblings will still fight. Sorry! This book will not cure all problems of teachers and parents! However, if a child begins learning soft skills at an early age, they will be more prepared to work with others and live harmoniously in the future.

Soft skills will help school-age children learn how to work more productively in school and will prepare them for skills such as organization and time management. They will help in college and vocational schools that will prepare them for future educational endeavors. Applying soft skills to an educational setting will allow parents and teachers to work together to teach students to be college and career ready. Soft skills will also prepare students

113

to grow and be productive, regardless of the format or environment in which they are learning.

Soft skills will prepare children for the world of future employment. As more and more employers are looking for applicants who are team players, have a positive attitude, and display integrity in their everyday work lives, soft skills will help prepare children for these qualifications as they apply to the work world as well.

Communication skills will help children be able to interact with others, share new ideas, and communicate feelings and concerns. They will teach children that listening to others and being aware of body language and nonverbal cues are also ways that kids and adults communicate in the real world.

Teamwork will help students learn how to work with others in a kind way, and to develop the skills necessary for the world of their future careers. By learning how to collaborate and cooperate, children will be more successful in sports, clubs, and other activities that prepare them for the future.

Manners help children learn kindness, compassion, and the skills needed to work with others. Children who have good manners show others that they are caring and kind people who know the social norms to be successful.

Like manners, *respect* is also an important skill for preparing children for the future. Children who are respectful of their peers and the adults in their lives will become workers who are admired and respected in the work world as well.

Empathy helps children learn how others feel and how they can help those who are experiencing problems or need some assistance. The skill of empathy allows children to see how their actions impact others, and how feelings can help them in the future.

Composure or maintaining control of one's emotions and anger will help children be successful both in school and the workplace. By learning how to maintain composure, children will be able to work through the tough times and be able to problem-solve ways to do so later in life.

Responsibility is important as it teaches children to do their part in both the home and school settings. By learning responsibility as children, they will be able to take this skill with them into future career and job skills as well.

Motivation is the drive to complete what one started and continue on—even though the road may be rough. Learning to be motivated will help in preparing children to be college and career ready.

Resilience is the idea of making it through the tough times, and being able to continue, even amid problems and concerns in one's life. Teaching children the soft skill of resilience provides them an invaluable tool to help them overcome obstacles in their future.

Integrity is the idea of doing what is right, even when no one is watching. Integrity is a skill that classrooms need, and future employers want in the workers of tomorrow.

Organization is important so that children know where their shoes are in the morning and their keys are as adults. However, it is also a skill that will help children benefit more from their education and be more prepared for the workplace.

Like organization, *time management* is also a needed skill for the success of children. Learning to make the most of one's time, use time wisely, and be able to follow plans and schedules is needed in future education settings and jobs.

Balance is also important as it keeps children in check and less stressed. People who can learn the soft skill of balance are able to complete school and work activities, while still having time for fun and relaxation.

Finally, a *positive attitude* will take one far in the success of work and school. Children who learn a positive attitude at an early age are those who will continue to use this skill in the future. People who have a positive attitude are not only fun to be around but are appreciated by co-workers and employers.

Overall, the soft skills in this book can be taught by teachers and parents beginning at a very early age. By taking the time and effort to teach these skills, adults show children that they care about their well-being and want them to be successful.

HOW SOFT SKILLS APPLY TO TEACHERS

Teachers can model and use soft skills in the classroom and online environments. By teaching children to communicate, be a team player, and learn organization strategies, they can engage students in a variety of activities that will enhance these skills in the classroom. Teachers play a huge role in making sure that children are prepared and ready for the future they will encounter. They are responsible not just for the content of books, but in making sure that the children they teach are good citizens and kind people.

Educators are role models for the children in their classrooms. They are being watched by children on a daily basis and their behaviors and attitudes, whether good or bad, are copied by the children they encounter. By being compassionate and approachable, teachers can let children know they care about their well-being as well as their preparedness for the future. They can make sure that children feel respected and learn responsibility, and that they know how to remain composed in rough times.

Teachers can also communicate with parents and families when a child is experiencing difficulty with peers or struggling with schoolwork. They can help form a plan for helping a child be successful and can help locate resources that are needed to assist a child. Teachers can also listen to parents when their children are feeling overwhelmed or experiencing too much homework. Teachers are important as they can help children in many ways beyond simply learning the school curriculum.

In conclusion, teachers play an important part in the development of soft skills in children. By using the teachable moments and spontaneous lessons that occur during the day, teachers can emphasize the soft skills as outlined in this book. Educators are busy people too. They have lesson plans to write, materials to prepare, and meetings to attend. However, realizing that taking a moment to listen to children, helping them learn a new soft skill, and giving them the tools to prepare them for the future is time well spent.

HOW SOFT SKILLS APPLY TO PARENTS

As stated in the previous chapters, parents play an important role in the development of soft skills in children. Parents are there from the start. They are a child's first teacher, a child's first role model, and the most consistent part of a child's well-being. Parents are there to nurture the scraped knees, the broken hearts, and the hurt feelings. They are also there to celebrate the milestones such as a child's first steps, losing a first tooth, and getting one's driver's license.

Parents start the foundation of a child's life, and provide the support, security, and guidance that are necessary to raise a child who has integrity and resilience. Parents can teach manners to children, guide them through learning teamwork, and help them develop empathy toward others. They can also work with other adults such as coaches and teachers to help a struggling child be more successful.

Families are important in teaching soft skills to help children achieve their goals and dreams and to prepare them for success in the school years and beyond. By having a supportive, caring, and safe home environment, children will see how others use soft skills and will be able to take these soft skills into their own futures.

Overall, parents have a huge responsibility to teach children to be well rounded, caring, and compassionate adults. Only by modeling proper behaviors, providing support, and encouraging students to be their best will this happen. Parents are important people, yet they are also busy people. Working on these skills a bit each day and taking advantage of *teachable moments* can help parents deal with the problems that children encounter, but also teach about dealing with successes in a humble and kind manner. By learning soft skills at an early age, children will be prepared with competencies needed to be successful at home, and in life.

THE FUTURE OF SOFT SKILLS IN
AN ONLINE SETTING

During the COVID pandemic, soft skills became an even more important tool for preparing children for the future. As students faced an increase in anxiety, schools had to re-examine how online teaching was delivered. Soft skills became a more important tool for the non-academic parts of teaching and will most likely continue in the future of online learning. According to Richards (2020b):

> In normal times, many schools didn't deliberately set aside time for teaching non-academic "soft skills" such as empathy, determination and self-care. That makes ramping up the focus in a virtual setting, amid a set of challenging circumstances, even more daunting.But the world is a stressful place right now, given the global health crisis, economic downturn and protests over racial injustice. It's important for school staff to nurture emotional connections, child psychologists and mental health experts say, even if addressing students' academic slide seems more urgent.

Teaching soft skills like responsibility and motivation can help students in an online environment and modeling skills such as organization and time management will help kids with the varied structure of virtual learning. By being aware of soft skills and applying them in an online setting, educators can build the proficiencies that students will need in their future, regardless of the format of the instruction.

Also, as schools made adaptations to online learning, the social emotional needs of students became more apparent to administrators and legislators alike. In a recent edition of *USA Today*, the following need was identified:

> Still, districts should not be judged on whether they were fast or slow to develop a plan. . . . What's more important, is whether the plan is developmentally appropriate, sensitive to the technological bandwidth people have in the homes, and responsive to the social and emotional needs of students and staff.

By being prepared and ready for soft skills in *any* educational setting, educators and parents will both see benefits of these skills in the kids with whom they are working.

THE FUTURE OF SOFT SKILLS AND CHILDREN

The world is constantly changing. New technology is created every day, and new skills and aptitudes are needed to help people be successful in their education and careers. Parents and teachers will need to be aware of the constantly changing needs of the world and be ready to learn and adapt curriculum and online skills to meet these ever-changing needs in children. However, some skills will be needed for any child, in any educational setting, and in any career choice.

Soft skills are the skills that will help children learn to be good people, work appropriately with others, and be prepared for future jobs. They are simple to teach and model and do not have to be taught in any certain order. Instead, they are taught as they are needed. When a child has a problem with a friend, then teach about teamwork and respect. When a student loses his homework or can't find assignments, then teach the skills of organization and time management. When a child is feeling overwhelmed, teaching the soft skills of composure and resilience can be helpful.

Being aware of the needs and concerns of the children in our lives and forming appropriate relationships with them is the best way to start. Parents who know the behaviors and actions of their children, and teachers who understand the needs and interests of their students will be able to assist children when a problem evolves. By knowing about the children in our lives, all adults can use soft skills to help them be better individuals and successful adults.

Soft skills are only a beginning to helping children learn to be the best people they can be. However, by having adults who are kind, nurturing, and caring, children will be more resilient and aware of the problems of the future.

Thanks to the many teachers and parents who will read this book and realize the importance of their role in the development of soft skills in children. The world is hard enough, but by learning soft skills now, children will be equipped with the necessary tools to help them be successful adults and future citizens.

Bibliography

Ajmera, Ripa. 2019. "How to Teach Children to Have Positive Attitudes." Accessed April 15, 2019. https://www.livestrong.com/article/77539-teach-children-positive-attitudes/.

Arora, Mahak. 2018. "Communication Skills for Kids: Importance and Activities to Improve." Accessed August 25, 2018. https://parenting.firstcry.com/articles/communication-skills-for-kids-importance-and-activities-to-improve/.

Bacher, Renee. 2019. "6 Ways to Motivate Your Kids." *Parents Magazine*. Accessed April 20, 2019. https://www.parents.com/kids/development/behavioral/6-ways-to-motivate-your-kids/.

Breaux, Annette. 2013. "Classroom Management Essential: Maintain Your Composure at All Times." Education World. Accessed April 10, 2019. https://www.education-world.com/a_curr/maintain-composure-classroom-management.shtml.

Buscaglia, Leo. (N. d.). "Loving Yourself Quote." Accessed April 8, 2019. https://www.goodreads.com/quotes/299651-to-love-others-you-must-first-love-yourself.

Cambridge Dictionary.com. 2019. "Definition of Self-Respect." Accessed April 8, 2019. https://dictionary.cambridge.org/us/dictionary/english/self-respect.

Dictionary.com. 2018. "Definition of Soft Skills." Accessed August 6, 2018. https://www.dictionary.com/browse/soft-skills?s=t.

Dictionary.com. 2019. "Definition of Resiliency." Accessed April 2, 2019. https://www.dictionary.com/browse/resiliency?s=t.

Education Week Research Center. 2016. *Mindset in the Classroom: A National Study of K-12 Teachers*. Bethesda, MD: Education Week.

Elkind, David. 1981. *The Hurried Child*. Boston: DeCapo Press.

Gallegos, Nina. 2019. "Encouraging a Positive Attitude by Creating a Positive Environment." Center for Parenting Education. Assessed April 15, 2019. https://centerforparentingeducation.org/library-of-articles/focus-parents/encouraging-positive-attitude-creating-positive-environment/.

Goldstein, Sam, and Robert Brooks, eds. 2014. *Handbook of Resilience in Children*. New York: Springer Publishing Company.

,Gopalan, Valarmathie Juliana Aida Abu Bakar, Abdul Nasir Zulkifli, Asmidah Alwi, and Mat Ruzinoor Che. 2017. *A Review of the Motivation Theories in Learning The 2nd International Conference on Applied Science and Technology 2017*

(ICAST'17), AIP Conf. Proc. 1891, 020043-1–020043-7. Accessed April 5, 2019. https://doi.org/10.1063/1.5005376.

Harvard Health. 2015. "The Importance of Recess." Accessed March 27, 2019. https://www.health.harvard.edu/exercise-and-fitness/the-importance-of-recess.

Indiana Senate Bill 297. 2018. "Employability Skills Curriculum. 2018." Indiana General Assembly. Assessed August 20, 2018. http://iga.in.gov/legislative/2018/bills/senate/297.

Kennedy-Moore, Eileen. 2014. "Time Management for Kids: Learning about Time Helps Kids Plan, Prioritize, and Work Productively." Accessed April 12, 2019. https://www.psychologytoday.com/us/blog/growing-friendships/201403/time-management-kids.

Kutner, Lawrence. 2018. "How Children Develop Empathy." Accessed August 5, 2018. https://psychcentral.com/lib/how-children-develop-empathy/.

Lewis, C.S. (N.d.). "Quote about Integrity." Accessed April 5, 2019. https://www.goalcast.com/2018/03/26/15-c-s-lewis-quotes/c-s-lewis-quote1/.

Loveless, Becton. 2021. *Teaching Soft Skills: The Complete Guide*. The Education Corner. https://www.educationcorner.com/teaching-soft-skills-guide.html

McQuerrry, Lisa. 2018. "Why Is Teamwork Important in the Classroom?" Accessed August 6, 2018. https://work.chron.com/teamwork-important-classroom-18281.html.

Mehrabian, Albert. 1980. *Silent Messages: Implicit Communication of Emotions and Attitudes*. 2nd Edition. Belmont, CA: Wadsworth Publishing.

Monster.com. 2018. "Soft Skills You Need." Accessed August 6, 2018. ttps://www.monster.com/career-advice/article/soft-skills-you-need.

Morin, Amanda. 2019. "4 Ways Kids Use Organization Skills to Learn." Accessed April 12, 2019. https://www.understood.org/en/learning-attention-issues/child-learning-disabilities/executive-functioning-issues/4-ways-kids-use-organiation-skills-to-learn.

Myers, Pam. 2019. "The Importance of Teaching Manners to Kids." Accessed March 25, 2019. https://childdevelopmentinfo.com/parenting/the-importance-of-teaching-manners-to-kids/.

National Association of School Psychologists. (2020). *Helping children cope with changes resulting from COVID-19*. https://www.nasponline.org/resources-and-publications/resources-and-podcasts/school-climate-safety-and-crisis/health-crisis-resources/helping-children-cope-with-changes-resulting-from-covid-19.

National Education Association (NEA). 2019. "Research Spotlight on Homework: NEA Reviews of the Research on Best Practices in Education." Accessed April 14, 2019. http://www.nea.org/tools/16938.htm.

Nemko, Marty. 2018. "Composure: Staying Calm but Focused Is an Underdiscussed Key to Career and Personal Success." Accessed April 2, 2019. https://www.psychologytoday.com/us/blog/how-do-life/201807/composure.

Nicholson, Pam. 2019. "Staying Calm During the Storm." Accessed April 10, 2019. https://centerforparentingeducation.org/library-of-articles/anger-and-violence/staying-calm-storm/.

Oxford Dictionary. 2019. "Definition of Balance." Accessed April 21, 2019. https://www.dictionary.com/browse/balance?s=t.

Price-Mitchell, Marilyn. 2015. "Integrity in the Classroom: How K-12 Teachers Influence Tomorrow's Ethical Leaders." Accessed April 9, 2019. https://www.psychologytoday.com/intl/experts/marilyn-price-mitchell-phd.

Proud to be Primary. 2019. "Teaching Responsibility in the Classroom: An Important Task." Accessed April 19, 2019. https://proudtobeprimary.com/teaching-responsibility-in-the-classroom/.

Richards, Erin. 2020a. "Historic Academic Regression: Why Homeschooling is So Hard Amid School Closures". Accessed August 5, 2021. http://www.usatoday.com/story/news/education/2020/04/13/coronavirus-online-school-homeschool-betsy-devos/5122539002/.

Richards, Erin. 2020b. "Kids' Mental Health Can Struggle During Online School. Here's How Teachers Are Planning Ahead." Accessed August 8, 2021. https://www.usatoday.com/story/news/education/2020/07/31/covid-online-school-kids-mental-health-teachers/5529846002/.

Quotabulary. 2018. "Encouraging Quotes for Kids to Shape Their Young Minds." Accessed February 1, 2019. https://www.google.com/url?q=https://quotabu-lary.com/encouraging-quotes-for-kids&sa=U&ved=0ahUKEwju8YOcvKXhAhWcnoMKHXP8ACUQFggFMAA&client=internal-uds-cse&cx=partner-pub-9037304895410090:8982596788&usg=AOvVaw2pXrIzegk9r0FnYiKweB_Y.

Shapiro, Susan. 2021. "5 Tips You Need to Know When Teaching Post-Pandemic." Accessed August 3, 2021. https://thejournal.com/articles/2021/07/29/5-tips-you-need-to-know-when-teaching-post-pandemic.aspx.

Spruce.com. 2019. "10 Most Important Benefits of Good Manners in Life." Accessed March 25, 2019. https://www.thespruce.com/how-you-benefit-from-proper-etiquette-1216688.

Stauffenger, Len. 2019. "4 Steps to a Balanced Life for Your Kids: Using a Sandwich." Accessed April 19, 2019. http://www.streetdirectory.com/travel_guide/201606/kids_and_teens/4_steps_to_a_balanced_life_for_your_kids_using_a_sandwich.html.

Talking Tree Books.com. 2019. "Definition of Respect for Kids." Accessed April 8, 2019. https://talkingtreebooks.com/definitions/what-is-respect.html.

Teach.com. 2019. "Motivating Students." Accessed April 3, 2019. https://teach.com/what/teachers-change-lives/motivating-students/.

UNICEF. 2019. "What Are Brain Breaks for Kids?" Accessed March 29, 2019. https://unicefkidpower.org/brain-breaks-for-kids/.

Van Buren, Abigail. (N.d.). "Quote About Responsibility." Accessed April 14, 2019. http://www.quotegarden.com/responsibility.html.

About the Author

Nancy Armstrong Melser is a mother, teacher, and author. Her first book *Teaching Soft Skills in a Hard World: Skills for Beginning Teachers* was published in 2018, and the next year *Soft Skills for Children: A Guide for Parents and Teachers* was published.

Nancy started her career as a first- and third-grade teacher as well as a gifted and talented educator. She is professor and director of transition to teaching at Ball State University, where she has taught for twenty-nine years. Nancy enjoys working with students in field experiences, student teachers, and those who have recently entered the teaching profession.

Nancy received her BA in elementary education from Indiana State University, and her MAE and EdD in elementary education and educational psychology from Ball State University. She grew up in a family of teachers and is dedicated to preparing students with real-life applications. She has a twenty□one-year-old son, Tyler, who has taught her a great deal about online learning through the eyes of a college student.

It is through Nancy's experiences as a teacher, mother, and mentor that she writes this book about soft skills for kids.

CPSIA information can be obtained
at www.ICGtesting.com
Printed in the USA
LVHW031821200223
739946LV00004B/461

9 781475 864892